Educational Research: Models for Analysis and Application

L. R. Gay

Florida International University

CHARLES E. MERRILL PUBLISHING COMPANY
A Bell & Howell Company
Columbus, Ohio

Published by
Charles E. Merrill Publishing Company
A Bell & Howell Company
Columbus, Ohio 43216

ISBN: 0-675-08600-0
Library of Congress Catalog Card Number: 75-40821

1   2   3   4   5 -- 80 79 78 77 76

Printed in the United States of America

To the Student

It is not unusual for a person to "understand" a concept or procedure in the abstract but not be able to apply it to a concrete situation. Comprehension is a necessary but not sufficient condition for application, analysis, synthesis and evaluation. The purpose of this book is to facilitate your transition from comprehension to these higher cognitive processes. Specifically, the objectives are:

1) to provide you with opportunities to self-test yourself so that you can evaluate whether you have achieved certain competencies; and

2) to provide you with models, or examples, which illustrate performances expected of you on Tasks.

The self-tests give you an opportunity to practice skills on which you will be ultimately evaluated. In most cases, several different practice examples are presented. It is to your advantage to do one example at a time. In other words, compare your response with the suggested response in the back of this book before going on to a second practice example. If your response is incorrect, study the suggested response, and if necessary reread the appropriate section of the corresponding chapter in the text (each chapter in this book corresponds to a chapter in the text). If you follow this suggested procedure, the second practice example will allow you to determine whether you have acquired the skill you were lacking when you attempted the first example. Third examples can be used as a double-check when you successfully perform on a first or second example, or they can be used as a self-check in the unlikely event that you are incorrect on both the first and second examples.

The Task examples which are presented were all developed by students in a beginning research course. As such, they do not necessarily represent "perfect" examples of research procedure but they do represent the level of performance expected of you at your current level of expertise. For example, by the time you get to Task 6 you should possess the knowledge and skill necessary to develop the method section of a research report which describes a study which could be conducted to test the hypothesis which you formulate in Task 2. To show how a problem is developed from Task to Task, the examples presented represent all the Tasks which were submitted for each of three diverse problems. Keep in mind that these Tasks were developed not by sophisticated researchers with 20 years of expertise, but by students just like you!

iii

Contents

1

Introduction to Educational Research

TASK 1-A

> Given a reprint of a research study, identify
> and briefly state:
>
> a)   the problem (purpose of the study),
> b)   the procedures,
> c)   the method of analysis, and
> d)   the major conclusions.

Enabler 1-A-1 calls for a listing and a brief description
of the major steps involved in conducting a research study;
the steps are described within the Chapter. Enabler 1-A-2
requires the same performance as Task 1-A; the only difference
is that you select the articles for Enabler 1-A-2. If you
can identify the stated components in articles of your choice,
you should be able to identify these components in an article
of your instructor's choice. Following this discussion, five
research reports are reprinted. Following each reprint,
spaces are provided for listing the components required by
Enabler 1-A-2 and Task 1-A. As a self-test, after you have
studied Chapter 1, select at least two of the reprints (any
two that look interesting to you) and see if you can identify
the components. If your responses match the Suggested Responses in the back of this supplement, you are ready for
Task 1-A. If your responses differ greatly from the Suggested
Responses, study the articles again until you see why you were

in error and then select two other articles and repeat the
process. If by some chance you incorrectly identify the
components of all five research reports, see your instructor.

Are Pupils in the Open Plan School Different?

F. S. WILSON
Toronto Board of Education

R. LANGEVIN
Clarke Institute of Psychiatry

T. STUCKEY
Ontario Institute for Studies in Education

ABSTRACT

Some educators have asserted that pupils in schools with "open plan" philosophies are superior to ordinary pupils in that they have more valued personality characteristics, mature faster, and have better attitudes toward education, as well as their environment. However, empirical evidence to corroborate these assertions is meager. This study compares pupils in two schools with open plan philosophies, to pupils from two traditional schools. Attitudes toward school, teacher, self, learning, and "school last year" were measured using a semantic differential. Pupils were also compared on measures of curiosity and productive thinking, or "creativity." It was found that open plan pupils have more positive attitudes toward school and themselves but there were fewer differences in the other concepts. There were no significant differences in measures of curiosity but differences in productive thinking occurred. Pupils who spent considerable time in an open plan school scored higher on some measures of productive thinking while pupils in a newer open plan school scored consistently less than a control group. The results were related to features of the open plan schools under consideration.

THE CONTEMPORARY open plan school is an evolution of Dewey's original proposals for progressive education. However, the concepts and philosophies of the open plan school have mushroomed in recent years so that there is no single philosophy or plan. Furthermore, while there are many schools advocating an open plan philosophy, there has been little research to assess the merits of such schools. The many claims and aims of these schools—permissiveness, self-discipline, originality, and curiosity—have not been assessed in any detailed way. The aim of the present study is to examine briefly two open plan schools and to see if some of these claims are valid.

Two schools with open plan philosophies[2] were investigated. Essentially the schools were non-graded and emphasized a discovery approach to learning (4).

The aim of a non-graded school is to diminish the sense of competition present in the graded school and to allow the child to proceed at his own rate. In such a school, retarded and genius are together with the average child. This presumably allows the child to advance at his own rate and to feel a greater sense of pride. In a study of a non-graded high school in Melbourne, Florida, Brown (3) pointed out two practical advantages: the percentage of dropouts fell and the number of college applicants increased when the school became ungraded.

Discovery learning, as advocated by Bruner, has received more experimental attention but the studies generally have been in laboratory settings (7, 8, 9, for example). The claims for discovery-learning have largely remained untested in the classroom and this is understandable since there are so many variables that enter into assessing one school or classroom versus another.

The discovery method presumably should have many advantages which are highly desirable in children. For one thing, the child is self-disciplined, he seeks out his own course of action and his own ways of learning which maximize his built-in potential and his existing methods of learning. One would expect that a child who is his own instructor will have a different self-image from a child who is the constant recipient of knowledge. One might also expect this child to attain a greater measure of self-control and maturity.

The second advantage of discovery learning is that the material the child studies has high interest value in that he is pursuing his own course of action and he is discovering the principles of various subjects by himself. In short, the discovery method is child centered and maximizes curiosity and originality. Research in creativity has suggested that curiosity, individuality or nonconformity, playfulness, self-confidence, and involvement in things are important features of the creative personality (1, 6, 10, 14). Thus, many of the features of the open plan philosophy aim to encourage these qualities in pupils. As part of an explicit program of self-discipline and development in the open plan schools, pupils are encouraged to do things for themselves and to interact with the teacher as a resource person rather than as an authority. The children are discouraged from raising their hands to ask questions but rather, to simply ask them in turn. They are expected to be responsible with materials and to show up for school on their own. Recess and lunch breaks are their own responsibility, and they often choose not to interrupt their activities to take recess or to go home at the end of the official school day.

Even the architecture of an open plan school conveys a sense of freedom. In one school under consideration there are few enclosed rooms; instead there are work areas for projects which are all at the periphery of a resource center and library. The emphasis is on large, open areas which contrast with the traditional space-confining classroom. The children are permitted free movement to and from the center and interact freely as they go. The purpose of the building plan is to make information easily accessible and to create a sense of independence. It also encourages self-discipline since a child may move freely and "waste his time" if he so chooses.

There is some difficulty in translating all the claimed advantages of an open plan school into operational terms. In addition, there are many important variables confounded in the school; it is non-graded, a discovery learning approach is used, and a program of self-development and self-discipline are explicitly used. The present study concentrated on three testable aspects of the claims: (a) the attitudes of the children to school and to themselves; (b) their level of curiosity; and (c) their level of productive thinking or "creativity," as measured by paper and pencil tests. If the school is operating effectively, the children should show (a) more positive attitudes toward school and themselves; (b) higher than average levels of curiosity; and (c) higher levels of productive thinking or "creativity."

Method

The Schools: Eleven and 12-year-old pupils from four schools in middle-class suburban Toronto took part in the study. The first school was a "lab" school, at the time of testing in operation for 6 years under the open plan philosophy. Of the total sample (N = 58), only nine Ss were new to the school the current year. While the school operated under the open plan philosophy, the building was a traditional school with separate classrooms and library with resource center. However, the students and faculty freely used all space at their disposal and it was not uncommon to see some project going on in the halls, gym, or staff commonroom.

The second open plan school was new at the time of testing, and in fact the pupils had only been established in their new building with the architecture described previously, in the latter part of the school year. However, pupils (N = 46) were treated under the open plan philosophy from the start of the year. The principal of the new school was former principal of the lab school. He and the new principal of the lab school held the same philosophy and consulted extensively. Many of the staff in this school were also former staff members of the lab school.

Two schools were used as control groups (N = 59). One school was a mixed fifth-sixth grade while the other was not. Both schools used a "traditional" classroom approach to teaching with the teacher directing activities and the pupils sitting in rows of desks. Subjects were taught textbook fashion with instruction and exercise. There were, however, features common to the open school—projects and field trips. The classes were graded and a discovery learning approach was not em-

ployed. Learning and activities were teacher-directed.

Materials. Three sets of materials were used: a semantic differential questionnaire to measure attitudes; the Torrance Minnesota Tests of Creativity to assess productive thinking; and two curiosity questionnaires, Specific Curiosity (5) and Reactive Curiosity (13) to assess curiosity.

The semantic differential was in the usual form described by Osgood (12). There were six concepts: books, learning, teacher, I, school, and school last year; and each was rated on twenty-one adjectives using a 7-point scale. The adjectives were: hard—soft, definite—uncertain, sharp—dull, sick—healthy, pleasing—displeasing, weak—powerful, small—large, complex—simple, interesting—boring, calm—exciting, ugly—beautiful, deep—shallow, passive—active, happy—sad, rough—smooth, good—bad, hazy—clear, hot—cold, meaningful—meaningless, relaxed—tense, likable—dislikable. The adjectives represent the three dimensions described by Osgood—potency, activity, and evaluation.

Four of the Minnesota Tests of Creativity were used: Product Improvement, in which the S is shown a picture of a toy dog and asked to write all the ways he can think of to improve the toy in order to make it more interesting for children to play with; second, Unusual Uses—Tin Can, in which the S is asked to produce unusual uses for a tin can; third, Figure Completion, in which the S is presented with a series of ten incomplete figures to complete in any way he pleases; finally, Circles, in which the S is presented with forty circles and is required to finish them in any way he chooses. Each test may be scored for fluency, flexibility, originality, and elaboration. In addition, Figure Completion and Circles may be scored for titles. Thus, there were eighteen measures in all.

The Specific Curiosity Questionnaire is a 36-item true-false test and the Reactive Curiosity Questionnaire is a 100-item true-false test with a built-in lie or validity scale. Both tests were administered together.

Procedure. All tests were administered in the usual school setting of the respective groups during regular school hours. Three separate periods were used to measure attitudes, curiosity, and creativity. Standard instructions and standard scoring were used in each case.

Results

Attitudes. The twenty-one adjectives for each concept were subjected to a one-way analysis of variance for the three groups: the lab school, new open plan school, and control group.[3] Mean scores for the three groups were compared using a Newman–Keuls Test with harmonic mean (15).

For the concept "school," all but two of the F-values were significant and in almost every case the means of the two open plan schools were not different from each other but both differed from the control group. In all cases, the attitude of the open plan pupils was more positive toward school than the attitude of the controls. School is more active, potent, and likable.

For "school last year," only two adjectives, complexity and roughness, differed significantly for the groups. However, the differences were marginal and this concept is not as meaningful as we originally expected, since most pupils were in the same setting as the previous year. Perhaps the only group this concept had meaning for was the pupils in the new open plan school.

The concept "I" showed some interesting differences, although all pupils showed positive self-regard. The open plan students saw themselves as sharper, more interesting, deeper, happier, and more likable. In short, they saw themselves as more potent than the controls did and they evaluated themselves more positively. However, the new open plan school pupils rated themselves as more definite, slightly better and clearer than the pupils of the control and lab school. This may be due to a combination of factors, the experience of their teachers, many of whom are from the lab school; the architecture and sense of freedom one gets from the building; or perhaps the sheer novelty of the experience.

The concept "books" showed some differences of interest. The open plan and lab school pupils saw books as more interesting and exciting than the control Ss but the new open plan Ss saw books as more definite, sharp, healthy, and pleasing than the other two groups. This difference may be again a novelty factor for the former group, since they were just discovering that they can read anything they want on school time. However, "books" was not considered central to a test of the effectiveness of the open plan school since children in any middle-class setting have usually been reinforced sufficiently, by the time they reach the age of our Ss, to like books. Furthermore, books are not necessarily associated with school.

"Learning" surprisingly showed few differences between the groups. Most of the evaluations were positive from all the groups and this is true of the concept "teacher" as well. However, in the case of teacher, it was expected that the individual personality of the teacher would be important. Most of the pupils seemed to like the teacher (the ratings were anonymous) in each of the groups.

In summary, the open plan students rated their school more positively and rate themselves more positively than the control Ss.

Curiosity and Creativity. A one-way analysis of variance was used to compare the three groups on two measures of curiosity and eighteen measures of creativity. There were no significant differences in curiosity among the groups.

All but two of the eighteen creativity measures showed significant differences in the groups.

However, in most cases the new open plan school showed the least creativity of the three groups. In five of the measures the lab school Ss were superior to the other two groups and in ten cases there was a trend to higher scores for the lab school. The lab school Ss were superior in verbal tasks.

The lower creativity scores were consistent across the tests for the new open plan school. A possible explanation is that the change in environment may be suppressing creativity, but eventually there is greater productive thinking as shown by the lab school. To test this hypothesis, amount of time spent in the lab school was correlated with creativity scores. Six of the eighteen correlations were positive and significant. Three of the largest correlations were on the Product Improvement task on which this group scored highest of all the schools. Thus, it may be that initially there is a suppression of productive thinking but with increased time in the open plan environment, "creativity" reaches a new high which is above average.

Discussion

The results generally confirm the claims that pupils in open plan schools have better attitudes toward school and toward themselves. There are other features of their behavior which were not assessed but which indicate their more positive attitudes. For example, one group recently voted to shorten the lunch hour in order to increase time spent on projects. Frequently, children pass up recess time to continue work and may work well past official closing time on their projects.

The higher levels of productive thinking in a continuing open plan environment show encouraging results for the open plan philosophy. The children in these schools are free to choose their own activities and these activities often take on a game or play form. This, in itself, is related to greater productive thinking (2). One may see a group writing poems, making mobiles, or building a maze to see "if their pet hamster can really learn to run it without error." Often "irrelevant" facts are brought into a conversation and incorporated into their activity. This is essential in the remote association theory of creativity (11).

Often children instruct children in the rules of a game or in the solution of a mathematical puzzle or on the breeds of fish in the aquarium. The teacher interacts with pupils in relation to their task and brings some concept or idea to the conversation. For example, when the teacher overheard a conversation about who took the water from the aquarium, he took the opportunity to explain evaporation. The children became most interested and set to work to measure evaporation accurately. It also served as a "lesson" in fractions and percentages. In another instance, a child became interested in a novel which he was reading during school time and mentioned this to the teacher. The teacher asked him what it was about, so that the conversation evolved into a "lesson" on plot, character, and evaluation of the book.

The pupils in the open plan schools demonstrate an obvious self-discipline, maturity, and absorption in their activities, even to a casual visitor. There is usually an expressed fear by parents that their children in the school will not "learn" anything and that they will be wild and waste time. In a large sample of photographs, there were practically no incidences where supervised and unsupervised students were not attending to some task.[4] Problem children are also rare. Generally they respond to the principle of respecting other children's privacy. For example, one boy bothering another might be told that it is unfair to interrupt another's work, and to either join him or go away. If a child is a pervasive problem, he may be told to go home if he does not like school. These problems were rare because the open plan philosophy advocates permissiveness not license. Many people fail to distinguish the two. The child is granted independence but he is not permitted to abuse it. These many factors are not easily measured by a paper and pencil test and methods are lacking to assess the complexity of what goes on in the classroom.

There were no differences among the three groups on curiosity measures. Since this study was completed, Langevin (10) found that curiosity is multifaceted and the Specific Curiosity Scale and the Reactive Curiosity Scale used in this study loaded on what could be called a breadth or diversive curiosity factor while important operational measures of curiosity such as exploration time and number of questions asked loaded on another factor, depth of curiosity or specific curiosity. Moreover, he found that only exploration time was significantly correlated with measures of creativity. Thus, the three groups in the present study may have differed in depth curiosity but not breadth curiosity or in the extent to which they engage in exploration.

Finally, a note of caution must be added to the encouraging results of the present study. There is always a problem in educational research of comparing schools. As in comparing personalities, it is possible that idiosyncracies play a part in the results. This cannot be ruled out in the present study. The principals and staff of the open plan school were enthusiastic advocates of the open plan philosophy. Our subjective impression was that they were atypical teachers and it is an open question whether the average teacher could function in such an environment. In some other so called open plan schools the traditional techniques have been imported into the open plan building and in one case there was even a partitioning into pseudo-classrooms. At the other extreme some advocates of the "open plan school" sat back and let the children "take over." When license reigned, their open plan school ended. Thus, it is not an easy task to operate a school with an open plan philosophy but the present study has suggested that when an open plan school is in proper operation it adds to contemporary educational goals.

FOOTNOTES

1. The authors wish to thank Dr. Hy Day for his advice on this study, and the principals and teachers of the schools for their cooperation.

2. Technically "open plan" refers to a form of architecture but "open plan philosophy," for lack of a better term, is used in this paper to mean the operation and aims of the school. "Open plan" unless otherwise specified, will mean the philosophy.

3. Tables of results may be obtained, upon request, from the senior author.

4. The authors wish to thank P. Legate and J. Bannister. They and the senior author photographed the children over the period of the school year. Pictures were taken in a pseudo-random fashion, aiming the camera where there were children, with no pre-plan.

REFERENCES

1. Barron, F., "The Psychology of Creativity," in Newcomb, T. (ed.), *New Directions in Psychology*, Vol. 2, Holt, Rinehart and Winston, Toronto, Canada, 1965.

2. Boersma, F.; O'Bryan, K., "An Investigation of the Relationship Between Creativity and Intelligence Under Two Conditions of Testing," *Journal of Personality*, 36:341–348, 1968.

3. Brown, B. F., *The Non-Graded High School*, Prentice-Hall, Englewood Cliffs, NJ, 1967.

4. Bruner, J., *The Process of Education*, Vintage Books, New York, 1960.

5. Day, H., "The Role of Specific Curiosity in School Achievement," *Journal of Educational Psychology*, 59: 37–43, 1968.

6. Day, H.; Langevin, R., "Two of the Necessary Conditions for Creativity," *Journal of Special Education*, 3:(no. 3)263–268, 1969.

7. Gagne, R. M.; Brown, L. T., "Some Factors in the Programming of Conceptual Material," *Journal of Experimental Psychology*, 62:313–321, 1961.

8. Kersh, B., "The Motivating Effect of Learning by Discovery," *Journal of Educational Psychology*, 53:65–71, 1962.

9. Kittell, J., "An Experimental Study of the Effect of External Direction During Learning on Transfer and Retention of Principles," *Journal of Educational Psychology*, 48:391–405, 1957.

10. Langevin, R., "A Study of Curiosity, Intelligence, and Creativity," unpublished PhD thesis, University of Toronto, 1970.

11. Mednick, S. A.; Mednick, M. T., "An Associative Interpretation of the Creative Process," in Taylor, C. (ed.), *Widening Horizons in Creativity*, Wiley, New York, 1964.

12. Osgood, C.; Suci, G.; Tannenbaum, P., *The Measurement of Meaning*, University of Illinois Press, Urbana, 1957.

13. Penney, R.; McCann, B., "The Children's Reactive Curiosity Scale," *Psychological Reports*, 15:323–334, 1964.

14. Torrance, E. P., "Scientific Views of Creativity and Factors Affecting Its Growth," in Kagan, J. (ed.), *Creativity and Learning*, Beacon Press, Boston, 1967.

15. Winer, B., *Statistical Principles in Experimental Design*, McGraw-Hill, Toronto, 1962.

Are Pupils in the Open Plan School Different?

The Problem

_____

_____

_____

The Procedures

_____

_____

_____

_____

_____

_____

_____

The Method of Analysis

_____

_____

_____

The Major Conclusion(s)

_____

_____

_____

The Objectives of Secondary School Chemistry Teaching as Reflected in Selected Professional Periodicals: 1918–1967

WILLIAM R. OGDEN, East Texas State University

MILTON O. PELLA, University of Wisconsin—Madison

ABSTRACT

The concern of this study is with the objectives for teaching secondary school chemistry stated in professional periodicals 1918–1967. The 1918–1967 period was divided into subperiods and selected periodicals were searched for statements of objectives. The statements found were first categorized as knowledge, process, attitude and interest, and cultural awareness. These categories were further subdivided on the basis of similarities and differences, into eighteen subclasses: five knowledge, three process, five attitude and interest, and five cultural awareness. Statements included in each of the subclasses were tabulated as to frequency of occurrence, category, authorship, and year of publication within each subperiod and across all subperiods. In addition to the above treatment, objectives considered to be "research-oriented" were studied separately. A background of historical facts served to establish an "intellectual climate" for each of the subperiods. This background consisted of a discussion of (1) the status of American education, (2) the growth of chemistry as a science, and (3) objectives noted in committee reports.

A CHRONOLOGICAL history of the objectives for teaching chemistry in the high schools of the United States during the period 1918–1967 is reflected by statements in articles from selected professional periodicals.

Chemistry is accepted as a science in most present day American secondary schools. Cubberley (4) called it the "mother of science instruction" in his *Public Education in the United States.* According to Ihde (10), chemistry has existed in the schools since before 1800, although for many years it was available mostly in connection with medicine or, on occasion, with mathematics. The best place for its acquisition was ". . . not in a university but in a pharmacist's shop."

A history of chemistry teaching in the United States was published in the *Journal of Chemical Education,* volume 9, number 4, which appeared during April of 1932. Lyman C. Newell (13) traced chemical education in America from earliest times until 1820, C. A. Browne (1) reported on the years from 1820 through 1870, Harrison Hale (7) characterized the 1870–1914 period, and F. B. Dains (5) reported on the 1914–1931 developments. While these articles contained some mention of high school chemistry, most of the emphasis was given to the development of the college course of study.

Histories involving secondary school chemistry have been attempted by a number of persons. Works by Clarke (2) and Powers (15) were primarily concerned with beginnings. Each traced the inception and growth of the subject from earliest times until the mid-1800's (Powers until 1850 and Clarke until 1880). A study by Rosen (16), part of a project which involved other sciences as well, analyzed developments in the public high schools during the 1820–1920 period. Two other studies, one by Fay (6) and one by Osborn (14), attempted to report on the entire range in time from the first appearance of the subject until date of publication (1930 and 1960 respectively).

Although the above mentioned histories are valuable for the information they impart, each contains its own bias. From the standpoint of the present study, none of them attempted to effectively deal with social, scientific, or educational issues which may have had an effect upon the teaching of chemistry during the time periods in question. Similarly, none of the above cited histories attempted to analyze the effect that periodical literature may have had upon teaching.

The present study attempts to build upon or extend those previously cited. While dealing generally with the history of chemistry teaching in the secondary schools of the United States during the 1918–1967 period, it is concerned with the question of the evolution of objectives as reflected by statements in articles from selected professional periodicals.

Studies by Hall (8) and Hurd (9) attempted to analyze trends in science education by utilization of a number of sources. Hall investigated chemistry teaching during the 1920–1938 period by selecting his data from committee reports, periodical literature, courses of study, and textbooks. Primarily concerned with biology teaching, Hurd utilized similar sources plus science education textbooks in determining 1895–1948 trends. Although both the Hall and Hurd studies involved

Reprinted from The Journal of Educational Research, 1974, 67(10), 472-480, by permission of the publisher and the authors.

analysis of periodical literature, neither gave primary consideration to this source, both limited their observations to relatively few journals, and Hurd utilized alternate year sampling procedures. The present study is an attempt to provide a greater insight as to what information pertaining to teaching objectives was available to the classroom teacher in the form of periodical literature during the 1918–1967 period.

Method

Step 1. Selection of Subperiods

The 1918–1967 period was divided into subperiods on the basis of selected events that were judged to have had an impact on the course of American educational history. In all cases some overlapping of subperiods was planned to allow for the gradual transformations characteristic of historical change.

While the selection of any dates to begin and end are arbitrary, the year 1918 is unique in that a number of significant happenings took place at that time. Kliebard (11) has cited the year 1918 as witnessing, among other things, the appearance of Franklin Bobbitt's *The Curriculum*, the first full length book on curriculum; William Heard Kilpatrick's "The Project Method," which appeared in *The Teachers College Record*, and was to have a wide influence on the activity movements of the 1920's and 1930's; and the report of the Commission on the Reorganization of Secondary Education entitled *The Cardinal Principles of Secondary Education*, which was to become a landmark in American educational history. In addition, 1918 saw the development of plans for the formation of the Progressive Education Association (3), the publication of a study by Wiley (17) entitled "An Experimental Comparison of Methods in Teaching High-School Chemistry" in the *Journal of Educational Psychology*, and the termination of World War I. Whereas the founding of the Progressive Education Association and the study by Wiley were of importance to education and the teaching of chemistry, the end of the war dramatically marked the end of one era and the beginning of another. Ihde has written that, following the close of World War I, leadership in chemistry began a shift from Germany, which had dominated the field before the hostilities, to Switzerland, Great Britain, and the United States. The year 1967 was chosen as the termination date because it represents the close of a 50-year period. In that most historical change does not take place in uniform intervals, it was decided to treat the 1918–1967 years in terms of subperiods of varying length rather than by decade or other equal time period. Individual subperiods are as follows:

Subperiod 1 (1918–1933). The first subperiod extends through 1933 since the effects of the 1929 depression were not expressly felt in education until the early 1930's. The year 1933 was selected to end the period because in that year the PEA undertook its 8-year study.

Subperiod 2 (1932–1941). The second subperiod extends from 1932, and the election of Franklin D. Roosevelt as President, through 1941 when the United States entered World War II.

Subperiod 3 (1939–1946). Subperiod 3 spans the 1939–1946 years, and covers the duration of World War II.

Subperiod 4 (1945–1957). Subperiod 4 extends from 1945 to 1957. It begins with the "Prosser resolution" and the following period of "life adjustment education" and ends with the successful launching of Sputnik I by the Soviet Union in 1957.

Subperiod 5 (1954–1967). The fifth subperiod begins in 1954 with a movement for re-evaluation of life adjustment education exemplified by an increase in the number of articles pertaining to shortages of American scientists and technicians and ends in 1967, the termination date of the study.

Subperiod 6 (1963–1967). While the 1954–1967 years are considered together as subperiod 5, those following 1962 (1963–1967), although included in subperiod 5, are thought of as the beginning of a new time interval (subperiod 6). The year 1963 was selected for a number of reasons: the assassination of President John F. Kennedy, a growing uneasiness with the first wave of post-Sputnik science curriculum projects as evidenced in the literature, and the appearance of the *Journal of Research in Science Teaching* which, unlike many before it, was dedicated to progress in science teaching through research. Although the terminal date for this subperiod is not known (1963–?), it is reported as 1963–1967.

Step 2. Collection of Data

A. Six periodicals were selected in an attempt to represent the literature available during the time period in question. The journals and dates of publication of each are listed below.

1. *School Science and Mathematics* (1918–1967)
2. *Science Education* and *The General Science Quarterly* (1918–1967)
3. *The Journal of Chemical Education* (1924–1967)
4. *The Science Teacher* and *The Illinois Chemistry Teacher* (1934–1967)
5. *The Bulletin of the Atomic Scientists* (1945–1967)
6. *The Journal of Research in Science Teaching* (1963–1967)

These periodicals were selected in order that articles of both the opinion and research types were represented. *School Science and Mathematics*, the journal of the Central Association of Science and Mathematics Teachers, and *Science*

Education were in existence during the entire 1918–1967 period although to 1929 *Science Education* was called *The General Science Quarterly*. *The Journal of Chemical Education*, of the American Chemical Society, was selected because of its devotion to chemistry. *The Science Teacher*, called *The Illinois Chemistry Teacher* before 1937, was selected on the basis of its wide circulation and affiliation with the National Science Teachers Association. *The Bulletin of the Atomic Scientists* was added to reflect post-1945 developments and *The Journal of Research in Science Teaching*, of the National Association for Research in Science Teaching and the Association for the Education of Teachers in Science, to show recent trends.

B. All issues of the periodicals selected were read for relevant articles. Articles were selected for re-reading upon the basis of the following criteria.

1. It was an expression of opinion or the result of formal research.

2. It was concerned with chemistry teaching at the secondary level. Articles concerned with science teaching in general were included if they used examples from chemistry or used general examples of use in the teaching of chemistry. Articles involving specific examples from subjects other than chemistry were eliminated.

3. It was concerned with chemistry teaching and not some phase of pure chemistry. Such "informational" articles were eliminated unless specific reference was made to the possible implications for teaching.

4. It was not a committee report or a critique of a committee report.

5. It was not an editorial or a letter to the editor.

C. Each article selected was abstracted as to its stated objectives and ideas expressed.

Step 3. Classification of Statements
A. *Pilot study.*—In an attempt to determine the workability of the project, a pilot study was undertaken in which 10 years were randomly selected from the 1918–1967 period. The ten corresponding volumes of *School Science and Mathematics* were systematically searched for titles concerned with high school chemistry teaching, high school science teaching, and the objectives of science teaching. The articles were read to determine the objectives advocated and the statements of objectives obtained were placed in tentative categories on the basis of similarities and differences.

Following this phase of the pilot study, selected articles were distributed to a panel of science educators. Each panelist was asked to identify the objectives advocated and to categorize each objective statement. Findings were compared and the following conclusions were made:

1. Objectives had to be stated explicitly. Implied objectives could not be considered.
2. Four categories (knowledge, process, attitude and interest, and cultural awareness) could be used.

B. *Categories of Objectives.*—Selected articles were read and re-read and statements obtained were classified within the four categories established. The statements were further subdivided within each category. During this phase of the investigation no attempt was made to duplicate the wording of the original authors. The subclassification was, instead, based upon common ideas or areas of concern such as "scientific methods of thinking," or "the nature of science and scientists." Categories and subclasses are defined as follows:

1. Knowledge objectives as determined from the data are these advocating the attainment of factual or conceptual material for its own sake or for its functional value and those stressing knowledges and skills basic to the study of chemistry. Types of objectives typical of this category are:

a. "Specific topics in chemistry"—Statements advocating the study of specifics such as ionization, equations and reactions, or atomic structure. Examples are those calling for the study of:
　　(1) ionization,
　　(2) valence,
　　(3) equation writing,
　　(4) the conductivity of fused salts, or
　　(5) the gas laws.

b. "Major facts, principles, concepts, or fundamentals"—Objectives of this type are less detailed than those relating to the study of "specific topics . . ." and usually involve more than one example. Examples of this type are:
　　(1) to teach principles or foundations,
　　(2) to develop understanding of fundamental facts,
　　(3) to distribute knowledge,
　　(4) to inculcate facts,
　　(5) to develop an understanding of principles and natural laws,
　　(6) to give broad training in fundamentals,
　　(7) to develop quantitative relationships,
　　(8) to develop conceptual schemes, or
　　(9) to cultivate general understandings.

c. "The applications of chemistry to daily life"—These objectives tend to call for the application of the concepts or fundamentals of chemistry to life situa-

10

tions and are specific in that examples are often provided. Examples of this objective stress:

(1) skill in applying the principles of chemistry,
(2) practical industrial or household uses of information,
(3) the ability to use chemistry to solve life problems, or
(4) intelligent consumership.

d. "A fund of useful information"—These objectives, although similar to c, stress the accumulation of a body of knowledge—not its application. Examples are:

(1) to give information of service to home and daily life,
(2) to acquire functional information,
(3) to give the student accurate scientific information, or
(4) to acquire a body of reliable and useful information.

e. "Study skills"—Objectives of this type tend to stress knowledges and skills necessary for the successful study of chemistry. They include use of proper nomenclature and vocabulary, mathematical skills, and study habits. Typical examples include:

(1) use of accepted nomenclature,
(2) the development of more exact terms to enlarge vocabulary,
(3) to develop the use of geometry in solving problems, or
(4) to encourage the use of applied mathematics.

2. Process objectives are those conveying an understanding and use of the methods and techniques of science. Statements included advocated skills in critical thinking and in problem solving as well as in the "processes" of observing, classifying, inferring, predicting, measuring, communicating, interpreting data, making operational definitions, formulating questions and hypotheses, experimenting, and formulating models (18). Types of objectives in this category are:

f. "Scientific methods of thinking"—These objectives deal with thinking skills and methods of thinking as outcomes of instruction in chemistry. Statements of this type tend to stress the development of critical thinking and problem solving abilities. Some examples are:

(1) to provide training in new ways of thinking,
(2) to stimulate thinking,
(3) to provide training in the scientific method of thinking,
(4) to develop the ability to reason,
(5) to improve thinking ability,
(6) to develop critical thinking,
(7) to give training in methodological thinking, or
(8) to encourage scientific thinking.

g. "Processes, skills, and techniques of inquiry"—Statements of this type are more functionally oriented than in f. They deal specifically with the techniques involved in employing the processes and methods of scientific problem solving. Examples are:

(1) to develop the ability to ask and answer questions,
(2) to observe accurately,
(3) to train in laboratory techniques,
(4) to develop skill in collecting and interpreting data,
(5) to develop skill in the use and handling of equipment, or
(6) to provide experiences in the process of getting information.

h. "Research and creativity"—These statements are concerned with developing the capacity to do research. As such, they differ from f and g in their degree of specificity and for this reason are considered alone. Typical examples are:

(1) to stimulate creative thinking,
(2) to do research,
(3) to teach creativity, or
(4) to develop the capacity for doing research.

3. Attitude and Interest objectives are those concerned with developing an appreciation of the contributions and nature of the scientific enterprise, desirable attitudes involving science and scientists, and lasting professional and avocational interests in students. Examples are:

i. "Scientific habits or attitudes"—Statements typical of this type of objective convey a willingness upon the part of the individual to use a scientific method of solving problems in everyday affairs. Aspects of the objectives are concerned with the formation of correct habits of thinking involving the ability and inclination to recognize a problem, consider evidence, suspend judgement, change an opinion, and other general indications of "scientific mindedness." Examples are:

(1) to develop scientific attitudes,
(2) to encourage the habit of using thought effectively in dealing with facts,
(3) to encourage the desire to know,
(4) to develop openmindedness,
(5) to provide for character for-

11

mation,

(6) to encourage scientific mindedness,

(7) to inculcate healthy attitudes, or

(8) to assist in the development of a value system.

j. "Appreciations"—These objectives carry an awareness and acceptance of the products and processes of science as they relate to life situations. They are on a more personal level than those involved with cultural implications and involve individual responses to the contributions of chemistry to daily living. Typical examples are:

(1) to develop an appreciation of the history of chemistry,

(2) to appreciate scientific and technological advances, or

(3) to develop an appreciation of the scientific method.

k. "Interest and hobby development"—Objectives of this type involve the development of non-career interests. Avocational pursuits such as photography or merely an interest in science reflected in a willingness to read about developments in chemistry are considered. Examples are:

(1) to encourage interest,

(2) to open new areas of interest and satisfaction,

(3) to encourage hobbies and leisure time activities,

(4) to maintain and promote interests, or

(5) to kindle enthusiasm.

l. "Career development"—Objectives relating to pre-professional or vocational training, such as those calling for the development of future scientists and technicians are treated separately from those concerned with interest or hobby development (k). The level of interest is more clearly specified and careers are definitely stated as the end product. Examples are:

(1) to find future scientists,

(2) to sell science,

(3) to encourage science as a means of livelihood,

(4) to give better vocational advice and choices,

(5) to help students develop aptitudes,

(6) to find and help the superior or gifted student,

(7) to develop and encourage vocational abilities,

(8) to provide vocational guid-

ance,

(9) to provide workers, or

(10) to develop future scientists and technicians.

m. "The nature of science and scientists"—Objectives of this type are concerned with the attainment of a realistic concept of the nature of science and scientists. Questions involving the workings and ethics or the scientific enterprise and those who make it function are central to this objective. Examples are:

(1) to develop an understanding of the nature of chemistry,

(2) to understand the philosophy of science,

(3) to show science as another human enterprise,

(4) to develop the understanding of science and its spirit,

(5) to provide for public knowledge of science,

(6) to understand what science is,

(7) to develop an awareness of the nature of science, or

(8) to comprehend the nature and ethics of science.

4. Cultural awareness objectives are those dealing with the interworkings of science and society or the cultural implications of science for society. Types of individual objective types are:

n. "Aesthetic aspects"—Objectives stressing the humanistic and creative aspects of science are considered to be of an aesthetic nature. Some examples are:

(1) to show science as a part of culture,

(2) to develop an understanding of the human aspects of chemistry,

(3) to show the humanizing aspects of chemistry,

(4) to explore the relationships between science and humanity,

(5) to teach the cultural values of science, or

(6) to show science as an aesthetic pursuit.

o. "Philosophical considerations"—Questions involving the ways in which science is influenced by the nature of society and the way science affects that society constitute philosophical objectives. Examples are:

(1) to develop a more intelligent understanding of the world,

(2) to show chemistry as a means of advancing civilization,

(3) to comprehend the contributions of chemistry to civilization.

(4) to show science as a means of social betterment, or

(5) to teach how chemistry brings about changes in the social order.

p. "Sociological implications"—Objectives involved with the effects of scientific innovations on society and their results are defined as sociological objectives. Examples are:

(1) to assist in social adjustments,

(2) to develop an understanding of the social implications of science,

(3) to understand the impact of science upon society, or

(4) to develop an understanding of the relationship between man and his environment.

q. "Economic aspects"—Awareness of how scientific advances influence economic development is considered to be a cultural awareness objective. Examples are:

(1) to show the economic implications of chemistry for mankind,

(2) to show how science creates an abundant life for all, or

(3) to show how chemistry has increased the standard of living.

r. "Political implications"—Objectives dealing with governmental policy as a result of scientific activity and those involving public support of science are thought to be of a cultural nature and are so classified. Some examples are:

(1) to teach chemistry in light of national needs,

(2) to teach the lessons of nature as a basis for democracy,

(3) to develop a responsible citizenry,

(4) to develop an educated electorate,

(5) to compete with Russia, or

(6) to develop public awareness of science.

Step 4. Analysis of Data

The information was analyzed to answer the following questions within and across subperiods.

A. What were the frequencies of articles and statements?

B. What was the distribution of objectives within each category?

C. Which objectives were the "most important"?

D. What were the frequencies of "research-oriented" articles and statements?

E. What major educational groups were involved with the writing of articles concerned with the objectives of secondary school chemistry teaching and did these groups agree or disagree in their outlook as indicated by frequency rankings?

Definitions

A. Secondary education is that planned for pupils in grades 9 through 12.

B. Chemistry is the first chemistry course in secondary school science.

C. Objectives are the stated outcomes, goals, or aims of instruction. The level of objective studied corresponds to what Krug (12) has termed "statements of instructional fields or school subjects."

D. Authorship is an occupational categorization of the authors of articles obtained from periodical literature. Such authors are considered as representing secondary education, higher education, or miscellaneous backgrounds.

E. "Research-oriented" objectives are those found in articles reporting the results of research activity.

F. "Most important" objectives are those accounting for 8.25 percent or more of the citations published during any one subperiod. (The figure 8.25 percent is arbitrary. The designation of a group of objectives as "most important" is intended to allow the convenience of discussing those objectives found to be among those most frequently cited during any one subperiod. The figure itself represents 1.5 times the 5.5 percent figure that would have been observed had all eighteen objective types been cited with equal frequency.)

Results

Although yearly fluctuations existed with respect to the numbers of articles and statements concerned with the objectives of secondary school chemistry teaching and the authorship of such articles and statements, it appears that:

A. Emphasis in terms of the most often cited objectives shifted from the knowledge category during subperiods 1–3 (1918–1946), through attitude and interest during subperiods 4 and 5 (1945–1967), to almost equal concern for all categories in subperiod 6 (1963–1967) (Figure 1).

B. Objectives relating to "scientific methods of thinking," "major facts, principles, concepts, or fundamentals," "specific topics in chemistry," "scientific habits or attitudes," "career development," "processes, skills, and techniques of inquiry," "the applications of chemistry to daily life," "sociological implications," and "the nature of science and scientists," in essentially that order, were found to be among the "most important" objectives for the teaching of secondary school chemistry during one or more of the six subperiods studied (Figure 2).

C. Most of the changes with respect to the objectives considered "most important"

13

occurred during subperiods 4, 5, and 6 (1945–1967) (Figure 2).

D. Following a low of 3.42 percent (down from 7.28 percent during subperiod 1) during subperiod 3, the frequency of "research-oriented" statements steadily increased to a high of 25.42 percent of all statements during subperiod 6.

E. The objectives most frequently published in conjunction with research activity were "major facts, principles, concepts, or fundamentals" during subperiod 1 (1918–1933),

Figure 1.—Categories of Statements of Objectives of Secondary School Chemistry Teaching Found in Periodical Literature Classified According to Subperiod, Percent of Statements, and Authorship: 1918–1967

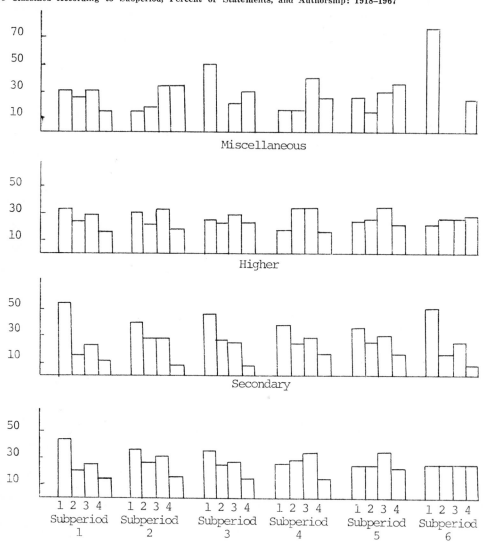

Subperiod and Categories
All Authors

CODE:
Subperiod 1: 1918–1933 (16 years)
Subperiod 2: 1932–1941 (10 years)
Subperiod 3: 1939–1946 (8 years)
Subperiod 4: 1945–1957 (13 years)
Subperiod 5: 1954–1967 (14 years)
Subperiod 6: 1963–1967 (5 years)

1—Knowledge objectives
2—Process objectives
3—Attitude and Interest objectives
4—Cultural Awareness objectives

Figure 2.—Distribution by Subperiod of the "Most Important" Types of Objectives for the Teaching of Secondary School Chemistry Found in Periodical Literature: 1918–1967

```
                                                                    f
    20                                                              f
                                                    f               f
                                                    f               f
                                                    f         f     f
 P  15   a          f i          f          f       f             b f
 e       a  f       f i       a  f          f       f             b f
 r       ab f       f i       a  f i        f     b f             b f
 c       ab f       f i       a  f i     a  f     b f  l          b f
 e       ab f       f i       ab f i     a  f  l  b f  l          b f
 n  10   ab f i     b f i      ab f i     ab f il  b f  l          b f    m
 t       abcf i     abcf i     ab f i     ab f il  b f  l          b f    m
         abcf i     abcfgi     abcfgi     ab fgil  ab f  lm        b f    mp
 o       abcf i     abcfgi     abcfgi     ab fgil  ab f ilm       ab f   lmp
 f       abcfgi     abcfgi     abcfgil    ab fgil  ab fgilm       ab f  ilmp
     5   abcfgil    abcfgil p  abcfgil p  ab fgil  ab fgilmp      ab fgilmp
 S       abcfgil    abcfgil p  abcfgil p  ab fgil p ab fgilmp     ab fgilmp
 t       abcfgil    abcfgil p  abcfgil p  abcfgilmp ab fgilmp     abcfgilmp
 a       abcfgil    abcfgilmp  abcfgilmp  abcfgilmp abcfgilmp     abcfgilmp
 t       abcfgil p  abcfgilmp  abcfgilmp  abcfgilmp abcfgilmp     abcfgilmp
 s       abcfgilmp  abcfgilmp  abcfgilmp  abcfgilmp abcfgilmp     abcfgilmp

         abcfgilmp  abcfgilmp  abcfgilmp  abcfgilmp abcfgilmp     abcfgilmp
         Subperiod  Subperiod  Subperiod  Subperiod Subperiod    Subperiod
             1          2          3          4         5             6
```

Subperiod and Objective Type
All Authors

CODE:
Subperiod 1: 1918–1933
Subperiod 2: 1932–1941
Subperiod 3: 1939–1946
Subperiod 4: 1945–1957
Subperiod 5: 1954–1967
Subperiod 6: 1963–1967

a—"Specific topics in chemistry"
b—"Major facts, principles, concepts, or fundamentals"
c—"The applications of chemistry to daily life"
f—"Scientific methods of thinking"
g—"Processes, skills, and techniques of inquiry"
i—"Scientific habits or attitudes"
l—"Career development"
m—"The nature of science and scientists"
p—"Sociological implications"

"scientific habits or attitudes" during subperiods 2 and 3 (1932–1946), and "scientific methods of thinking" during subperiods 4–6 (1945–1967).

F. The three author groups did not always think alike with regard to objectives. In general, authors from secondary education backgrounds favored knowledge while those from higher education backgrounds favored attitude and interest types. Authors in the miscellaneous group tended, during subperiods 2, 4, and 5, to cite objectives in the attitude and interest and cultural awareness categories most frequently (Figure 1).

Conclusions

Education for "social efficiency," the depression, competition with "New Deal" administrators regarding the custodianship of youth, World War II, "cold war" pressures, "life adjustment education," the Sputnik scare and the space race, civil rights, the new left, and the youth movement of the 1960's were factors which shaped education during the 1918–1967 years. As part of the curriculum of the American secondary school, the subject of chemistry and its teaching were undoubtedly affected by involvement in such issues.

Chemistry teaching was also vastly influenced by developments in the science of chemistry. Whereas prior to World War II the high school course was taught with a primary emphasis upon knowledge, an impression of chemistry itself, the post-1945 years saw more and more a reflection of the technological and theoretical improvements stimulated by the war effort. Increasingly the post-war years reflected an emphasis in process,

15

attitude and interest, and cultural awareness objectives.

The study generally supports the findings of Hall and Hurd (8, 9). Hall's work, published in 1938 and involving post 1920 high school chemistry, noted a trend toward meeting social needs which had the effect of ". . . broadening the base of the aims and objectives of high school chemistry." Although the present study does not acknowledge the appearance of new objectives in the literature of the 1930's that were not present in the literature of the 1920's, it is true that statements stressing process, attitude and interest, and cultural awareness objectives were more frequent during subperiod 2 than during subperiod 1, while those concerned with knowledge were less frequent. With regard to subclasses, greatest increase was with objectives calling for the development of "scientific habits or attitudes" and the greatest decrease with those concerned with the study of "specific topics in chemistry."

Hurd's study, involving trends in secondary school science teaching, acknowledged training students in the scientific method of thinking to be the most important objective during the 1895–1948 period. The present study would verify this observation with respect to the 1918–1948 years and extend it through 1967. His observations with respect to objectives stressing the development of scientific habits or attitudes is also well taken. Such objectives were found to be most frequent during the 1930's.

Hurd also noted that only five objectives (out of the twenty-six he had identified) accounted for all citations during the 1941–1948 years. Although there is not a direct relationship between Hurd's objectives and those of the present study, his contention is not supported. Analysis of the literature of the same period revealed statements pertaining to seventeen of the eighteen objectives identified ("research and creativity" was not cited). While the lack of a one to one correspondence between objectives in the two studies is again noted, the discrepancy might best be accounted for by the fact that Hurd consulted only two journals (actually only one prior to 1930) and utilized alternate year sampling procedures in his collection of data. The present study utilized six journals (five during the 1941–1948 years) and consulted all volumes.

Although this study does not mean to suggest that the objectives cited as prevalent in the literature were actually incorporated in the classrooms, it is believed that an adequate body of information reflecting concern for the development of good secondary school chemistry teaching was available to the classroom teacher during the years in question. It is not the objective of this study to produce a complete history of science education, or even of secondary school chemistry for that matter. It is hoped, however, that this investigation and others like it, will, in time, lead to the development of such a history.

REFERENCES

1. Browne, C. A., "The History of Chemical Education in America Between the Years 1820–1870," *Journal of Chemical Education*, 9:677–695, 1932.
2. Clarke, Frank Wigglesworth, *A Report on the Teaching of Chemistry and Physics in the United States*, United States Bureau of Education Circular of Information, No. 6–1880, Government Printing Office, Washington, D. C., 1881.
3. Cremin, Lawrence A., *The Transformation of the School*, Vintage Books, New York, 1961.
4. Cubberley, Ellwood P., *Public Education in the United States*, Houghton Mifflin, Boston, 1934.
5. Dains, F. B., "Advances in the Teaching of Chemistry Since 1914," *Journal of Chemical Education*, 9:745–750, 1932.
6. Fay, Paul J., "The History of Chemistry Teaching in American Schools," *Journal of Chemical Education*," 8:1533–1562, 1931.
7. Hale, Harrison, "The History of Chemical Education in the United States From 1870–1914," *Journal of Chemical Education*, 9:729–744, 1932.
8. Hall, Carrol C., "Trends in the Organization of High School Chemistry Since 1920," *School Science and Mathematics*, 38:766–772, 1938.
9. Hurd, Paul DeHart, "A Critical Analysis of the Trends in Secondary School Science Teaching From 1895–1948," unpublished PhD Dissertation, Leland Stanford Junior University, 1949.
10. Ihde, Aaron J., *The Development of Modern Chemistry*, Harper and Row, New York, 1964.
11. Kliebard, Herbert M., "The Curriculum Field in Retrospect," in P.W.F. Witt (ed.), *Technology and the Curriculum*, Teachers College Press, New York, 1962.
12. Krug, Edward A., *Curriculum Planning*, Harper and Brothers, New York, 1957.
13. Newell, Lyman C., "Chemical Education in America From the Earliest Days to 1820," Journal of Chemical Education, 9:677–695, 1932.
14. Osborn, Gerald, "Chemistry in the Secondary Schools of America," *School Science and Mathematics*, 60:621–625, 1960.
15. Powers, Samuel Ralph, *A History of the Teaching of Chemistry in the Secondary Schools of the United States Previous to 1850*, The University of Minnesota, Minneapolis, 1920.
16. Rosen, Sidney, *A History of Science Education in the American Public High School, 1820–1920*, unpublished PhD Dissertation, Harvard University, 1955.
17. Wiley, William H., "An Experimental Study of Methods in Teaching High School Chemistry," *Journal of Educational Psychology*, 9 (no. 4):181–198, 1918.
18. Wisconsin Department of Public Instruction, *A Guide to Science Curriculum Development*, WDPI, Madison, 1968.

The Objectives of Secondary School Chemistry
Teaching as Reflected in Selected
Professional Periodicals: 1918-1967

The Problem
_____

_____

_____

The Procedures
_____

_____

_____

_____

_____

_____

_____

_____

The Method of Analysis
_____

_____

_____

The Major Conclusion(s)
_____

_____

_____

Immediate Knowledge of Results and Test Performance

RICHARD O. BEESON,[1] **University of Arkansas**

ABSTRACT

Three groups of students used IBM card punchboards to receive immediate knowledge of results after each of one-half of the items' on multiple-choice tests and received delayed knowledge of results on the remaining items. Two-way analysis of variance was used to test for significant differences in the results under the two conditions on each of ten 1-hour examinations and on a final examination. There were no statistically significant differences in means under immediate and delayed knowledge of results on any of the 1-hour examinations. The difference in results on the final examination, however, was significant beyond the .05 level in favor of immediate knowledge. Immediate item-by-item knowledge of results thus did not depress test performance.

THE NECESSITY for change in conventional testing techniques is supported by research (2, 4, 6). One possible change incorporates a most important aspect of programmed learning or self-instructional devices: immediate knowledge of results (KR). The importance of KR as a means for more efficient learning also is supported by research (1, 3, 5), but it is not known whether KR generally depresses or increases scores when students are given immediate knowledge of their performance after each test item. Virtually no attention has been paid to this potentially useful testing technique. The purpose of this study was to investigate the possible effect of KR on test performance.

Method

The samples used in this study consisted of three groups of mathematics students. Group I consisted of thirty students enrolled in a university class in mathematics for elementary school teachers; Group II consisted of fifteen students enrolled in a university class in remedial mathematics; and Group III consisted of thirty students enrolled in a junior high school class in general mathematics. Students were randomly assigned to either one of two subgroups within their respective group. Once a student was assigned to a subgroup, he remained with that subgroup throughout the experiment. One subgroup in each group received KR on either the first or second half of the items on the test. The other subgroup in each group received the opposite condition. Each subgroup had delayed knowledge of results (DKR) on the other half of the test items. No subgroup received KR on the same half of the test items on any two consecutive tests. Care was taken to assure that KR on an item in one part of a test did not cue the answer to an item elsewhere in the test.

Group I used the punchboard as a self-instruc-tional as well as a testing device. They were given brief orientation and practice in its use prior to each 1-hour examination. There were four 1-hour examinations and four practice tests. The latter did not count toward final grades. The conditions with respect to KR and DKR were the same for the practice as for the 1-hour tests. Group I also used the punchboard on their final examination.

Groups II and III were each given brief orientation and practice sessions in the manipulation of the punchboard, and used it on each of three 1-hour examinations.

Scores were recorded for each student on each half of the test for the respective condition under which that part of the test was administered. The score for the KR condition was the total number of correct responses in one attempt. The score for the DKR condition was the total number of correct responses on that half of the test.

Results

The means and standard deviations for KR and DKR for each group are shown in Table 1. Two-way analysis of variance was used to determine the effect of KR on student test performance. The .05 level of significance was used. The statistical model was the mixed model, with rows being individuals and columns being treatments. Because this was a mixed model with N = 1, no meaningful test for row effects was possible. The results of the two-way analysis of variance for KR and DKR for each examination for each group are shown in Table 2.

One can observe from Table 2 that there were no statistically significant differences in student performance when given KR and when given DKR on any one of the ten 1-hour examinations. The difference in the results of the two testing methods on the one final examination, however, was significant beyond the .05 level in favor of KR.

Reprinted from The Journal of Educational Research, 1973, 66(5), 224-226, by permission of the publisher and the author.

18

Table 1.—Means and Standard Deviations for KR and DKR

Exam	Variable	Group I Mean	Group I SD	Group II Mean	Group II SD	Group III Mean	Group III SD
1	KR	14.53	2.47	8.27	1.33	12.83	3.75
	DKR	14.00	2.89	7.67	1.78	11.67	3.82
2	KR	15.83	2.52	7.60	2.16	12.83	4.32
	DKR	16.10	3.36	7.00	1.77	11.40	4.44
3	KR	12.73	3.63	6.47	2.31	10.23	3.92
	DKR	12.80	3.17	6.07	3.21	10.63	4.14
4	KR	13.43	3.75				
	DKR	12.63	4.07				
Final	KR	28.97	6.08				
	DKR	27.27	6.38				

Table 2.—Analysis of Variance for KR and DKR

Group	Exam	Source	df	MS	F
	1	Columns	1	4.27	2.140
		Residual	29	1.99	
I	2	Columns	1	1.07	0.346
		Residual	29	3.07	
	3	Columns	1	.07	0.011
		Residual	29	4.51	
	4	Columns	1	9.60	1.100
		Residual	29	8.24	
	Final	Columns	1	43.35	4.620
		Residual	29	9.38	
	1	Columns	1	2.70	1.465
		Residual	14	1.84	
II	2	Columns	1	2.70	0.950
		Residual	14	2.84	
	3	Columns	1	1.20	0.272
		Residual	14	4.41	
	1	Columns	1	20.42	3.402
		Residual	29	6.00	
III	2	Columns	1	30.82	3.388
		Residual	29	9.09	
	3	Columns	1	2.40	0.208
		Residual	29	11.54	

19

Discussion

From the statistical analyses of the data, it was concluded that in general, there were no significant differences in the results of the two methods of testing. Although the F ratios for the 1-hour examinations did not reach significance at the .05 level, there were some differences worthy of mention. An investigation of Table 1 reveals that the overall performance was slightly higher when students were given KR. The difference in results in the analysis of variance for the 1-hour examinations and the final examination bears further comment. It is important to note that student performance was not lessened by KR; rather, it was improved generally by being given KR, even on the 1-hour examinations. Perhaps the increased length of the final examination over each of the 1-hour examinations accounts for the fact that the F reached the .05 level of significance. This suggests that significant differences might have resulted on the 1-hour examinations if they had been longer, more reliable examinations. This thesis finds added support in the fact that students tended to perfom better when they were given KR.

The findings appear to justify recommending that classroom mathematics teachers make greater use of testing devices which give students immediate item-by-item knowledge of results.

FOOTNOTE

1. Now at St. Louis University. The author wishes to thank Edward J. Furst, University of Arkansas, for his assistance.

REFERENCES

1. Angell, G. W., "The Effect of Immediate Knowledge of Quiz Results on Final Examination Scores in Freshman Chemistry," *The Journal of Educational Research*, 42:391–394, 1949.
2. Angell, G. W.; Troyer, M. E., "A New Self-Scoring Test Device for Improving Instruction," *School and Society*, 67:84–85, 1948.
3. Little, J. K., "Results of Use of Machines for Testing and for Drill upon Learning in Educational Psychology," *The Journal of Experimental Education*, 3:45–49, 1934.
4. Pressey, S. L., "A Simple Apparatus Which Gives Tests and Scores—and Teaches," *School and Society*, 23:373–376, 1926.
5. Willey, C. F., "Classroom Scoring of Tests," *Psychological Reports*, 4:611–617, 1958.
6. Willey, C. F., "The Punchboard in Group-Decision Testing," *Psychological Reports*, 20:1209–1210, 1967.

SELF-TEST FOR TASK 1-A

Immediate Knowledge of Results and
Test Performance

The Problem

_____

_____

_____

The Procedures

_____

_____

_____

_____

_____

_____

_____

The Method of Analysis

_____

_____

_____

The Major Conclusion(s)

_____

_____

_____

THE ONE-MINUTE STEP TEST AS A MEASURE OF 600-YARD RUN PERFORMANCE

Joan E. Manahan and Bernard Gutin

This study investigated the validity of several different types of step tests in predicting the ability of ninth grade girls to perform the 600-yard run. The Skubic-Hodgkins test, in which heart rate is taken 60–90 seconds after stepping up at 24 steps per minute for three minutes, was given. Recovery heart rates from 5–20 and 25–40 seconds postexercise were also taken. The other tests utilized required the subject to give an allout effort. Total repetitions completed constituted the score. These were one- and two-minute two-count step-ups and one- and two-minute four-count step-ups. The three recovery heart rates were significantly (.05), but not closely, related to the 600-yard run time (r's of .399, .325, and .344 for 5–20, 25–40, and 60–90 seconds postexercise, respectively). All four allout step tests were much more closely related to 600-yard run performance (r's ranging from —.718 to —.824). Test-retest reliability coefficients were determined for the two one-minute tests, which were most closely related to running performance. Reliability coefficients were .698 for the four-count test and .952 for the two-count test. It was concluded that the one-minute, two-count step-up test is a valid and reliable measure of 600-yard run performance in junior high school girls.

THE AAHPER (1) AND THE FLEISHMAN (3) fitness batteries include the 600-yd. run. Because of problems with weather and facilities which may make it difficult to administer this test, it is desirable to have available other valid and reliable tests which can be substituted for the 600-yd. run. In this way the individual teacher may be able to choose a test which meets the criterion of practicality for a particular situation, as well as the criteria of validity and reliability.

Step tests have the virtue of requiring very little in the way of space or equipment. These tests generally involve having all subjects step up at the same rate for a specified period of time with the recovery heart rate (HR) taken for some period postexercise (2, 4, 6). Two difficulties arise in this kind of test. First, it is difficult to keep all subjects stepping at the specified rate. If a person is unable to continue stepping at the specified rate for the entire test he is supposed to be stopped and the recovery period started at that point. Thus it becomes difficult to administer the test to several students concurrently, since each tester really needs his own stop watch to time the recovery period. Related to this problem is the fact that the person's score must be calculated in a formula which considers both the time spent stepping and the recovery HR. It is very difficult to combine these factors into a score which is on the same scale as scores based only on recovery HR. Another weakness of this kind of test is the need to have testers who can count HR accurately. Although students can be

Reprinted from The Research Quarterly, 1971, 42(2), 173-177, by permission of the publisher and the authors.

trained to do this, there is bound to be some unreliability built into this measurement, especially with younger students.

Step tests which require the student to step as many times as possible within a specified time period would seem to require a type of capacity similar to that found in distance running. Furthermore, the counting of completed step-ups is within the capability of even relatively young students, thereby facilitating the testing of large groups by arranging students in pairs and having them count for each other.

This study was designed to determine the validity of various step tests as measures of 600-yd. run performance in ninth grade girls. Those tests which provided the best prediction of performance were then studied further for reliability and the effects of age, weight, and height.

Method

Subjects. Ninth grade girls (N = 40) enrolled in regular physical education classes in Bloomfield, New Jersey, served as subjects. Their ages, heights, and weights are summarized in Table 1.

TABLE 1
DESCRIPTIVE STATISTICS FOR 40 SUBJECTS

	Mean	SD	Range
Age (months)	171.7	5.2	160–188
Height (inches)	63.7	2.2	59.5–68.8
Weight (pounds)	119.1	18.2	87–176

Tests

1. *600 yard run-walk.* Four subjects at a time ran twice around a rectangular area which was 290 by 160 ft. As a girl crossed the finish line, the number of seconds were called out by the timer and then recorded. The subjects were paired off, with one girl noting the time while the other girl ran.
2. *Skubic-Hodgkins step test.* An 18-in. bench and a metronome set at 96 beats/min. were used, resulting in 24 steps/min. Subjects performed two at a time for 3 min. Subjects sat down and three recovery pulses were taken 5–20 sec., 25–40 sec., and 60–90 sec. postexercise, by palpation of the carotid artery by two physical education teachers. A subject was stopped if she could not keep the pace for a 15-sec. period.
3. *One- and two-minute (four-count) step test.* An 18-in. bench was used. Four subjects were tested at a time. They had to step up and down in four counts to perform a complete step-up. The lead leg could be alternated. Emphasis was placed on extending the legs and back on the step-up and subjects were not permitted to jump down from the bench. Four ninth grade students acted as counters.

23

4. *One- and two-minute (two-count) step test.* As in the four-count step tests, an 18-in. bench was used and four subjects were tested at a time. Four ninth grade students acted as counters. The counter held hands with the subject throughout the test as a safety precaution. Subjects were directed to start with the right foot on the bench, to straighten the right leg and back, and not to place the left foot on the bench. Instead they were to return the left foot to the floor, repeating this procedure as many times as possible in the time period allowed. When the lead foot became fatigued the subject was permitted to change feet.

Results and Discussion

The correlation coefficients between the various step-up test scores and the 600-yd. run time are presented in Table 2[1]. The three postexercise heart rate measures were significantly related to 600-yd. run time ($P < .05$). Subjects with lower postexercise heart rates tended to have lower times in the run. This relationship was somewhat closer if the heart rate was taken immediately postexercise rather than allowing some recovery to take place, as prescribed in the Skubic-Hodgkins procedure. In any case, the correlations were not high, heart rates accounting for no more than 16% (R^2) of the variance in the run scores. On the other hand, correlations between the allout step tests and running time were fairly high, with the two-count 1-min. test accounting for 68% of the variance in running times ($r = -.824$). Thus the use of this step test to predict 600-yd. run scores is more than four times as accurate as using postexercise heart rate.

Since the four-count and two-count 1-min. step test seemed to be the most valid predictors of 600-yd. run time, test-retest reliability coefficients were determined for these tests. For the four-count test the coefficient

TABLE 2
SUMMARY OF CORRELATIONS BETWEEN STEP-UP TESTS AND
SCORES ON THE 600-YARD RUN

Step-up test	r
Skubic-Hodgkins Test	
5- to 20-second recovery pulse	.399[a]
25- to 40-second recovery pulse	.325[a]
60- to 90-second recovery pulse	.344[a]
Two minute (four-count)	−.718[b]
Two minute (two-count)	−.764[b]
One minute (four-count)	−.783[b]
One minute (two-count)	−.824[b]

[a] Significant at .05 level
[b] Significant at .01 level

[1] One subject, who weighed 176 lb., did not complete the 3-min. step test. Therefore she was not included in the correlations involving the postexercise heart rates.

found was .698, and for the two-count test it was .952. Thus the two-count 1-min. test was found to be both the most valid and reliable test of those studied. The superior reliability of the two-count test may be attributed to two factors. First, the scores are more precise because one repetition is counted for each two beats rather than for each four beats. Second, in the four-count test it is difficult to determine the difference between a fast step-down and a jump down, which is not permitted. In the two-count test one leg is always kept on the bench, thereby obviating the problem of students jumping rather than stepping down.

Scores of the two-count 1-min. test were then correlated with height, weight, and age. The correlation with height was not significant ($r = .135$). Skubic and Hodgkins (5) and Sloan (7) also found that height was not significantly related to step test scores. The correlation with weight was also nonsignificant ($r = -.276$). Although all subjects in this study were in the ninth grade, there was some variability in age. Therefore step-up scores were correlated with age, taken to the nearest month, and a significant r of .358 ($P < .05$) was found. However, a close inspection of these data indicated that the older subjects in this study tended to be those who had also received higher grades in physical education. Therefore it is not clear at this point whether age must be considered in developing norms for this test. Skubic and Hodgkins (4) have indicated that on their test age was not a significant factor in females of junior high school through college age.

Conclusions

The two-count 1-min. step test is a reasonably valid and reliable measure of 600-yd. run performance in junior high school girls. This test lends itself well to group testing in a gymnasium, thereby providing a practical indoor alternative to the 600-yd. run.

References

1. American Association for Health, Physical Education, and Recreation. *Youth fitness test manual.* Washington, D.C.: the Association, 1961.
2. BROUHA, L., and GALLAGHER, J. R. A functional fitness test for high school girls. *Journal of Health, Physical Education, Recreation* 14:517-50, December 1943.
3. FLEISHMAN, EDWIN. *The structure and measurement of physical fitness.* Englewood Cliffs, N.J.: Prentice-Hall, 1964.
4. SKUBIC, VERA, and HODGKINS, J. Cardiovascular efficiency tests for girls and women. *Research Quarterly* 34:191-98, May 1963.
5. ———. Cardiovascular efficiency test scores for college women in the United States. *Research Quarterly* 34:454-61, December 1963.
6. ———. Cardiovascular efficiency test scores for junior and senior high school girls in the United States. *Research Quarterly* 35:184-91, May 1964.
7. SLOAN, A. W. Effect of training on physical fitness of women students. *Journal of Applied Physiology* 16:167-69, January 1961.

The One-Minute Step Test as a Measure of
600-Yard Run Performance

The Problem

_____

_____

_____

The Procedures

_____

_____

_____

_____

_____

_____

_____

The Method of Analysis

_____

_____

_____

The Major Conclusion(s)

_____

_____

_____

Reality can indeed be disturbing—particularly if it taps assessment of the reading and awareness of qualified English personnel. Through a questionnaire technique, Mr. Hipple and Mr. Giblin sampled selected professional reading behavior of 386 English teachers in the state of Florida. Although their rate of return was only 67%, the randomness of the returns suggests an adequate basis for their conservative interpretations. While the fineness of discrimination between journal titles might account for some of the responses, the implications for the preparation of English teachers, teacher education in general, in-service programs, and dissemination of information is only too apparent.—Reviewed by W. R. P.

The professional reading of English teachers in Florida

THEODORE W. HIPPLE
University of Florida

and THOMAS R. GIBLIN
*University of Colorado,
Colorado Springs Center*

The practicing secondary school English teacher in Florida is not likely to be engaged in much professional reading related either to education in general or to teaching English in particular. Furthermore, his university preparation has not been remarkably rich with professional reading experiences. Though blunt and unflattering, these generalizations appear inescapable after one studies the results yielded in a survey designed to test the knowledge English teachers have of educational journals and books.

In May, 1970, a survey of reading habits was sent to 580 randomly selected teachers of English in the state of Florida.

From Research in the Teaching of English, 1971, 5(2), 153-164. Copyright © 1971 by the National Council of Teachers of English. Reprinted by permission of the publisher and the authors.

The survey listed six journal titles related to the teaching of English, ten journal titles related to education, and 20 book titles in each field. Also included was a numbering system enabling respondents to indicate the degree of their familiarity with the works listed.

As a precaution against a teacher's checking items whether he had read them or not, exactly half of the journal and book titles listed were fictitious. (In this report the imaginary titles are printed in lower case; in the actual survey, of course, all titles were printed alike. See Tables 3–5.) The anonymous survey also solicited information about the respondents' education and teaching experience and about their membership in professional organizations.

Of the 580 sent, 386 completed and usable surveys were returned. On these returns, the failure of the fictitious title to attain wide mention attests to the validity of the results received. Had, for example, the Langley title (a fictitious one) outranked the Hook title or the Moffett title (both real), then the entire set of results might have been rendered suspect. It appears that, for the most part, the respondents were honest, even though such integrity revealed a distressing lack of acquaintance with what has been written about education generally and English teaching specifically.

THE SAMPLE   The selection of the approximately 580 teachers of secondary school English in the state of Florida to whom the survey was sent was facilitated through the offices of either the county supervisor of language arts or the county representative of the Florida Educational Research and Development Council, a statewide organization. This person was asked to distribute the survey sheets sent to him to randomly selected secondary school English teachers within his county district. The returns indicated that the desired randomness was attained, with completed and usable surveys coming from 48 counties in Florida. Though the instrument permitted no exact way of checking whether all the returned surveys from one county came from one school (and, hence, from one English department), this appeared not to be the case, as reported by the differences in school populations identified on surveys returned from those counties which have more than one secondary school.

Randomness was further indicated by the education and experience of the teachers who completed the survey. Of the responding teachers, 37% (125) possessed a master's degree or higher, 63% (261) a bachelor's degree. There were no returns from teachers who had not earned at least a bachelor's degree. Moreover, the experience levels of the respondents ranged from one year to 36 years. These figures are shown in Table 1.

Table 1
Years of Experience and Education of Respondents

	1–3	4–7	8–12	13–18	over 18 years	Totals
B.A.	88	62	42	27	42	261
M.A.	16	20	22	32	35	125
						386

Participation in professional organizations reflected another dimension of the variety of the survey population. Questions were asked about membership in four organizations, two national and two state: The National Council of Teachers of English (NCTE), the National Education Association (NEA), the Florida Council of Teachers of English (FCTE), and the Florida Education Association (FEA). The results are summarized in Table 2.

Table 2
Membership in Professional Organizations

	NCTE	NEA	FCTE	FEA
B.A.	119	107	128	110
M.A.	76	66	85	70

THE RESULTS   Part II of the instrument sought information about the reading of journals related to the teaching of English in particular and to education in general. As explained above, exactly half of the titles listed in the survey were fictitious. The data yielded is presented in Table 3. (Fictitious titles are indicated in lower case print; real, in upper case.)

Part III of the instrument questioned respondents about their familiarity with books related either to the teaching of English or to education in general. Table 4 presents the information received about the reading of books dealing with the

Table 3
Readership in Professional Journals

Meanings of Response Code Numbers
1. I have never heard of this journal.
2. I am slightly familiar with this journal, but do not recall reading it.
3. I once used this journal some, but no longer read it.
4. I do not subscribe to this journal, but do read it occasionally.
5. I do not subscribe to this journal, but do read it regularly.
6. I subscribe to this journal, but seldom read much of it.
7. I subscribe to this journal and read it regularly.

Name of Journal	1	2	3	4	5	6	7	Degree
The Composition Teacher	148	68	15	28	2	0	0	B.A.
	61	40	5	18	1	0	0	M.A.
ELEMENTARY ENGLISH	92	107	28	27	3	0	4	B.A.
	40	45	16	20	1	2	1	M.A.
THE ENGLISH JOURNAL	7	12	16	67	53	13	93	B.A.
	0	6	4	27	20	3	65	M.A.
English News and Notes	164	50	6	31	7	0	3	B.A.
	68	30	8	12	4	0	3	M.A.
MEDIA AND METHODS	78	49	25	52	27	3	27	B.A.
	25	23	7	30	22	1	17	M.A.
Secondary School English	90	70	25	61	13	1	2	B.A.
	45	30	15	27	6	0	2	M.A.
Classroom Digest	177	54	10	15	5	0	0	B.A.
	86	21	7	9	1	0	0	M.A.
CLEARING HOUSE	144	62	20	29	3	2	1	B.A.
	45	25	16	18	8	2	1	M.A.
Contemporary Issues in	171	57	5	25	1	0	1	B.A.
Secondary Education	80	23	7	14	0	0	1	M.A.
Education in America	166	67	7	15	4	0	2	B.A.
	77	31	4	13	0	0	0	M.A.
JOURNAL OF SECONDARY	112	76	17	49	4	0	3	B.A.
EDUCATION	48	33	19	22	3	0	0	M.A.
PHI DELTA KAPPAN	143	71	13	28	4	1	1	B.A.
	44	37	9	17	8	3	7	M.A.
SCHOOL AND SOCIETY	172	52	8	27	2	0	0	B.A.
	62	21	17	22	3	0	0	M.A.
Secondary School Teaching	136	76	15	30	4	0	0	B.A.
	67	31	6	19	2	0	0	M.A.
TODAY'S EDUCATION	28	32	26	54	18	11	82	B.A.
(formerly NEA JOURNAL)	8	11	17	16	11	8	54	M.A.
Today's High Schools	167	47	9	32	6	0	0	B.A.
	79	25	6	16	2	0	1	M.A.

teaching of English. (Again, fictitious titles are presented in lower case.)

Table 4
The Reading of Books about the Teaching of English

Meanings of Response Code Numbers:
1. I have never heard of this book.
2. I have heard of this book, but have not read any of it.
3. I have read parts of this book.
4. I have read all of this book.
5. I have studied this book carefully and feel that I know it rather well. (If you own any of these books, please add a "6" to the number already in the blank.)

Author and Book Title	1	2	3	4	5	6	Degree
Allanson: English for all American	225	21	6	0	0	0	B.A.
Youth	102	17	5	0	1	0	M.A.
Brauer and Snead: Composition	161	51	47	2	1	2	B.A.
in the English Class	74	21	23	6	1	1	M.A.
BURTON: LITERATURE STUDY	113	38	57	24	29	28	B.A.
IN THE HIGH SCHOOLS	30	15	37	13	30	23	M.A.
Clark: English for Democratic	224	28	9	1	0	1	B.A.
Living	98	19	6	2	0	0	M.A.
COMMISSION ON ENGLISH OF	166	35	37	12	12	9	B.A.
THE CEEB: FREEDOM AND	58	19	15	12	21	13	M.A.
DISCIPLINE IN ENGLISH							
Committee of Nine of the NCTE:	115	49	65	25	8	7	B.A.
A Guide to the Teaching of English	39	26	37	14	9	4	M.A.
DIXON: GROWTH THROUGH	196	44	15	5	3	1	B.A.
ENGLISH	80	20	14	6	5	6	M.A.
EVANS AND WALKER: TRENDS	149	50	48	14	2	3	B.A.
IN THE TEACHING OF ENGLISH	66	27	23	5	4	3	M.A.
Fryaan: Language Teaching and	214	24	23	1	0	0	B.A.
Language Learning	85	25	12	2	1	0	M.A.
GUTH: ENGLISH TODAY	191	37	21	6	8	3	B.A.
AND TOMORROW	77	27	15	3	3	2	M.A.
Hendrick: English during the	202	30	25	4	3	2	B.A.
Secondary School Years	87	23	12	2	1	0	M.A.
HOOK: THE TEACHING OF	91	34	62	20	57	51	B.A.
HIGH SCHOOL ENGLISH	30	10	32	22	31	26	M.A.
Langley: The Teaching of High	139	51	52	15	8	8	B.A.
School Literature	70	16	25	7	6	3	M.A.

Author and Book Title	1	2	3	4	5	6	Degree
MOFFETT: A STUDENT-CENTERED LANGUAGE ARTS CURRICULUM, K–13	169	46	28	12	9	9	B.A.
	68	28	23	1	5	2	M.A.
MULLER: THE USES OF ENGLISH	179	43	26	8	8	11	B.A.
	79	17	22	4	3	4	M.A.
Pierce and Anderson: English in Grades 7–12	211	29	17	1	6	4	B.A.
	101	14	10	0	0	0	M.A.
ROSENBLATT: LITERATURE AS EXPLORATION	190	33	33	5	4	2	B.A.
	79	23	17	4	2	2	M.A.
Steelman: Poetry for Secondary School English Study	172	40	35	40	8	5	B.A.
	85	21	16	3	0	0	M.A.
THOMAS: TRANSFORMATIONAL GRAMMAR AND THE TEACHING OF ENGLISH	92	55	75	22	20	21	B.A.
	49	17	35	10	14	13	M.A.
Willard: The study of English	218	26	20	1	1	2	B.A.
	97	13	11	4	0	0	M.A.

Table 5 presents the information received on books dealing with education in general.

Table 5
The Reading of Books about Education in General

Meanings of Response Code Numbers:
1. I have never heard of this book.
2. I have heard of this book, but have not read any of it.
3. I have read parts of this book.
4. I have read all of this book.
5. I have studied this book carefully and feel that I know it rather well. (If you own any of these books, please add a "6" to the number already in the blank.)

Author and Book Title	1	2	3	4	5	6	Degree
Atkins: The Society of the Secondary School	224	27	10	2	2	1	B.A.
	100	14	8	0	1	0	M.A.
BARZUN: TEACHER IN AMERICA	191	33	28	5	7	5	B.A.
	55	28	25	11	4	4	M.A.
BLOOM: TAXONOMY OF EDUCATIONAL OBJECTIVES	136	15	67	21	23	20	B.A.
	43	18	36	13	13	9	M.A.
Brown and Standish: The Dynamic of Secondary Education	225	20	7	1	0	0	B.A.
	97	17	7	1	1	1	M.A.
BRUNER: THE PROCESS OF EDUCATION	172	31	39	12	10	7	B.A.
	61	21	23	6	11	7	M.A.

Author and Book Title	1	2	3	4	5	6	Degree
CONANT: THE AMERICAN	77	26	84	46	34	21	B.A.
HIGH SCHOOL TODAY	11	13	41	31	27	16	M.A.
Dorsey: Adolescents and	196	37	24	3	3	1	B.A.
Their Schools	85	19	16	1	1	0	M.A.
Fellows: Teaching for Maturity	223	29	10	1	0	0	B.A.
	96	21	5	0	0	0	M.A.
FRIEDENBURG: THE	186	45	19	6	6	5	B.A.
VANISHING ADOLESCENT	74	24	15	3	6	3	M.A.
HOLT: HOW CHILDREN FAIL	120	48	52	23	20	13	B.A.
	40	24	23	28	8	4	M.A.
HIGHET: THE ART OF	160	33	50	10	10	8	B.A.
TEACHING	59	22	18	10	13	10	M.A.
Jarrett: High School: Teacher,	218	24	18	3	0	0	B.A.
Pupils and Programs	81	19	20	2	0	0	M.A.
Knowland: The Uses and Abuses	217	31	10	5	1	0	B.A.
of the Schools	94	22	6	1	0	0	M.A.
LEONARD: EDUCATION AND	212	33	11	4	3	0	B.A.
ECSTASY	85	21	11	3	2	3	M.A.
MAYER: THE SCHOOLS	218	26	12	5	2	1	B.A.
	90	17	11	3	2	3	M.A.
Neilsen: The Science of Teaching	215	83	13	2	0	0	B.A.
	95	12	16	0	0	0	M.A.
Olney: Educational Objectives in	106	53	77	16	16	8	B.A.
Secondary Education	48	26	31	13	5	1	M.A.
POSTMAN AND WEINGARTNER:	183	45	23	5	7	6	B.A.
TEACHING AS A SUBVERSIVE	71	29	12	8	3	5	M.A.
ACTIVITY							
Saunders: Democratic Education in	234	22	5	2	0	0	B.A.
Autocratic Schools	108	12	3	0	0	0	M.A.
Tichenor: Subject-Matter Teaching	210	30	19	2	2	1	B.A.
in Student-Centered Classes	86	25	9	2	1	1	M.A.

SOME 1. Some of the English teacher respondents identified jour-
ANALYSES nals and books which do not even exist as ones they had read;
e.g., Langley's *The teaching of high school literature* was reported as read by 113 respondents and owned by 11 of these
teachers. If one is tempted, however, to conclude from these
data that the respondents were dishonest, he may be doing
them a disservice. While it is possible that some of the teachers checked imaginary titles as ones they were familiar with

simply to enhance the picture of their professional reading, it is equally possible that some of the teachers who made such indications were simply mistaken. Book titles in education have a remarkable similarity, and a teacher could rather easily confuse an imaginary book with a real one he had read a few years earlier. A teacher with several years of experience, for example, might recall having read a particular book for an education course eight or ten years earlier; a title listed on the survey might *seem* to be the title of the book he had read. Hence, he identified it as one he had read. A student of these data cannot, in short, infer universal duplicity when there exists such a forceful potential for simple and honest error.

Then, too, the events of the moment may have influenced many teachers. The most widely studied imaginary book was Olney's *Educational objectives in secondary education*. At the time the teachers completed this survey, most were involved in yearlong statewide work on behavioral objectives. Doubtlessly many of them had studied some printed materials on such objectives (very possibly Mager's *Preparing instructional objectives*) and concluded, quite honestly even if mistakenly, that the Olney title was the one they had examined. Again, then simple error and not deliberate fabrication caused these data.

Nonetheless, one's charitable assertion of error must not hide what surely exists to some degree: the purposeful distortion by a few teachers of this report of their professional reading habits and libraries. No less than teachers in other disciplines, some teachers of secondary school English view with a sense of self-guilt the paucity of their professional reading. Quite naturally, they hope to appear better read than they are. Even though the survey was kept anonymous, even though the results of a particular teacher's responses never reached his superiors but were sent directly to the authors, no doubt some teachers wanted to seem well-read, a condition easily achieved by the expedient of marking a "3" or "4" where a "1" or "2" would have been more truthful. It follows that such teachers would reveal themselves occasionally with their indications of substantial familiarity with imaginary journals and books.

2. Of course, the really pertinent data concern the familiarity teachers have with journals and books which do exist, and here the picture is somewhat depressing. For whatever reasons (and a few of these will be examined in the con-

clusion to this section) teachers of secondary school English are not presently reading widely in professional literature, nor have they read widely in the past. A few exceptions to these generalizations stand out, notably the *English Journal* and *Today's Education* among the journals and works like Burton's, Hook's, and Conant's among the books. Even these, however, need further examination.

The *English Journal* and *Today's Education* are membership bonuses, respectively, of the National Council of Teachers of English and the National Education Association. When one joins these organizations, he automatically receives these journals. Comparison of Tables 2 and 3 reveals that membership in these organizations does not, however, automatically insure the careful reading of the journals. Of the 185 belonging to the NCTE, only 158 used a "7" to indicate thorough reading of the *English Journal*.

Among the books, Burton's *Literature in the secondary schools* was one of the most popular. Professor Dwight M. Burton has for many years been a professor in and chairman of the Department of English Education at Florida State University, the largest teacher-training institution in Florida. It is highly probable that more than a few of the Florida teachers who completed this survey studied at FSU, possibly under the direction of Professor Burton himself. Moreover, Professor Burton has been very active in the state of Florida, working tirelessly for better English teaching. In short, his name is well-known among Florida English teachers. The popularity of his book may, therefore, be at least somewhat a function of the geographical area in which the survey was conducted.

J. N. Hook's *The teaching of high school English* has been the most popular of the "methods" texts used in undergraduate methods courses, almost since its initial edition in 1950 (it is now in its third edition). A person who elects to teach English is typically required to take a methods course; not infrequently the book studied will be Professor Hook's.

The most popular of the general books was James Conant's *The American high school today*. Here, too, there is reason to question the validity of its popularity, as Conant's book achieved that rarity among books about education: it attained "best seller" status. Its popularity among the responding English teachers may be owing somewhat to its popularity with the general public and may be of limited inferential use as an indication of the amount of professional reading engaged in by English teachers.

In no way should these remarks be construed as disparagement of these three books. All three are excellent works and deserve widespread readership. The more distressing finding, in fact, is that despite the foregoing explanations, there are substantial numbers of responding teachers who have not heard of these books: 133 had not heard of Burton's book, 121 were ignorant of Hook's, 88 were unaware of Conant's.

3. As with these three books, the overall lack of readership of some of the journals and books merits further attention. *Media and Methods* has been on the cutting edge of innovation in the English classroom for the last several years, perhaps more than any other single source. This significant journal has been largely responsible for the advocacy and legitimization of media study in the English classroom. Yet 103 of the responding teachers had never ever heard of the journal and another 72, though they had heard of it, had never seen a copy. Of those magazines which direct their attention to education in general (as opposed to the first list of journals, which primarily are slanted toward the teaching of English), none except the aforementioned *Today's Education* had any substantial following among the respondents to this survey.

With books, the situation is much the same. For example, Rosenblatt's *Literature as exploration* was unknown to 269 teachers. Yet it is the work about which James R. Squire, former executive secretary of the National Council of Teachers of English, writes "It is one of the very few books on the teaching of English that I believe all teachers should read." The reports of the Anglo-American Conference on the Teaching of English fared no better. This extraordinary gathering of scholars in English, English education, drama, linguistics and psychology from the British Islands, Canada, and the United States met at Dartmouth College in 1966 and engaged in penetrating and intelligent discussion of the issues which face English teachers. Called the Dartmouth Seminar, this important conference authorized two different summaries of its proceedings: Dixon's *Growth through English*, a work intended for members of the profession, and Muller's *The uses of English*, a work intended for the lay public but useful also to teachers and other professionals. Of the 386 respondents, 276 had never heard of Dixon's work, 258 of Muller's.

Another work regarded as of substantial importance by scholars in English and English education was the report *Freedom and discipline in English,* issued by the Commission on English of the College Entrance Examination Board; it, too, had small readership, with 224 respondents unfamiliar even with the title.

Examination of the data with respect to general books in education reveals a reading lack similar to that demonstrated in the books more closely related to the teaching of English. Older but still relevant and useful works like Barzun's *Teacher in America* and Highet's *The art of teaching* were no more popular than more recent works like Holt's *How children fail* or Postman and Weingartner's *Teaching as a subversive activity.* The numbers of respondents who had not heard of these works are, respectively, 246, 219, 160, 254.

4. When possible, observations should go beyond a mere repetition of the results to include some judgments about the causes of the particular data received. The dominant question about the yield of this survey is, Why have these teachers read so little in these important journals and works? One answer, of course, centers on the sample, that its randomness resulted in the selection of ill-prepared teachers who have made little attempt to keep professionally up-to-date. Such an inference does an injustice to the many teachers among the respondents who have read widely. Furthermore, the very randomness of the sample suggests that these teachers differ little from their counterparts all over the country. Each teacher surveyed had at least a bachelor's degree from an accredited teacher-training institution. One must, therefore, look beyond the group of respondents to ascertain the answer to the question of the limited professional readings.

In all likelihood the answer lies in the nature of the English teacher's job. On the one hand, the English teacher works long and hard hours simply to keep on top of his duties. Typically, he teaches five classes comprising approximately 150 students. He has lessons to prepare, tests to construct, and, above all, compositions to correct. A 300-word theme from each of his students represents, in total, the same amount of reading as in an average sized professional book. Some English teachers, rightly or not, receive themes this long from each of their students *each week.*

On the other hand, what reading time the English teacher

has must be apportioned among several competing areas of concentration. As a student of literature he feels a continuing obligation to read the Dickens novel or the Ibsen play he has not yet read; he must also read criticism of this literature. But he cannot ignore the contemporary best sellers which his abler students are reading, perhaps on loan from their parents. Nor can he ever forget his need to study that literature written especially for the adolescents whom he teaches daily; the latest novel by Betty Cavanna may be the answer to motivating Susan, who simply will not read. Finally, and that is precisely the place it achieves among the reading priorities of many English teachers, comes professional reading, the study of those journals and books related to teaching English in particular and to education in general. It is not that these teachers find professional reading to be valueless; it is, often, that their time is too limited and that other areas of reading seem to them to merit their first attenion. Also, as this study suggests, many English teachers are simply unaware of what exists in professional literature.

Attempts to find the "why" of limited professional reading, however, must not obscure the obvious need to discover methods through which English teachers can become more familiar with educational literature. Though such methods are beyond the scope of this report of research, English educators, both those training prospective teachers and those engaged in in-service work with practicing teachers, must still seek new ways to encourage professional reading.

SELF-TEST FOR TASK 1-A

The Professional Reading of English
Teachers in Florida

The Problem

_____

_____

_____

The Procedures

_____

_____

_____

_____

_____

_____

_____

The Method of Analysis

_____

_____

_____

The Major Conclusion(s)

_____

_____

_____

TASK 1-B

>Given reprints of three research studies,
>classify each as historical, descriptive,
>correlational, causal-comparative or experi-
>mental research and list the characteristics
>of each study which support the classifica-
>tion chosen.

Enabler 1-B-1 calls for definition and identification
of major characteristics of each of the five methods of research; definitions and characteristics are described within
the Chapter. Enabler 1-B-2 entails description of three
possible research studies for each of the five methods of
research. You are to "make them up," rather than find them
in journals. Chapter 1 includes a number of examples for
each of the methods. Reread each of those examples before
attempting to write your own. After you have completed
Enabler 1-B-2, for each example ask yourself the questions
presented within the section of Chapter 1 entitled Guidelines
for Classification. If the answers to those questions suggest
that each example does indeed represent the method of research you intended it to represent, you are in business (that
means you are probably ready for Task 1-B). As a self-test,
classify by method the preceding research reports; use the
form which follows. If all your choices and reasons agree
with the Suggested Responses, you are definitely ready for
Task 1-B. If you miss one, make sure you understand why you
were in error. If you miss several, and especially if you do
not understand why, see your instructor.

SELF-TEST FOR TASK 1-B

Are Pupils in the Open Plan School Different?

Method:_____

Reasons:_____

_____

_____

_____

_____

The Objectives of Secondary School Chemistry
Teaching as Reflected in Selected Professional Periodicals:
1918-1967

Method:_____

Reasons:_____

_____

_____

_____

_____

Immediate Knowledge of Results and Test Performance

Method:_____

Reasons:_____

_____

_____

_____

_____

The One-Minute Step Test as a Measure of 600-Yard Run Performance

Method:_____

Reasons: _____

_____

_____

_____

_____

The Professional Reading of English Teachers in Florida

Method:_____

Reasons: _____

_____

_____

_____

_____

2

Selection and Definition of a Problem

TASK 2

> Write an introduction for a research plan.
> This will include a statement of the specific
> problem to be investigated in the study, a
> statement concerning the significance of the
> problem, a review of related literature, and
> a testable hypothesis. Include definitions of
> terms where appropriate.

Enablers 2-1 to 2-4 involve the selection of a problem,
identification and annotation of related references, and
formulation of a research hypothesis. Since in succeeding
chapters you will be performing Tasks as they relate to your
problem, you should give careful thought to the selection of
a problem. Also, since the research competencies required
for the conduction of an experimental study include many of
the competencies required for conduction of studies representing the other methods of research, and more, it is to your advantage to select a problem which can be investigated experi-
mentally; you will acquire experience with a wider range of
competencies and should be able to generalize many of those
competencies as they apply to the other methods of research.
Task 2 involves the writing of an introduction to a research plan which follows the guidelines described in Chapter
2. Following this discussion, three examples are presented
which illustrate the format and content of such an introduction. These examples, with few modifications, represent Tasks

submitted by former students in an introductory research course. Examples from published research could have been used, but these examples more accurately reflect the performance which is expected of you at your current level of research expertise.

THE COMPARATIVE EFFECTIVENESS OF PARENT AIDES VERSUS SALARIED PARAPROFESSIONALS IN THE KINDERGARTEN CLASSROOM[1]

INTRODUCTION

Individualized instruction is a priority in education today. Many teachers, however, find it to be an impossibility due to class size and time consuming non-professional duties. Recognizing this problem, an increased number of trained and salaried paraprofessionals have been hired by school systems to free teachers of duties which do not require professional competency. In many schools, the lack of funds for trained and salaried paraprofessional aides has led administrators to organize pools of volunteer parents to aid teachers in achieving individualized instruction.

Statement of the Problem

The problem to be investigated in this study is the comparative effectiveness of the use of volunteer parents as teachers' aides versus salaried and trained paraprofessional aides in the kindergarten.

Review of Related Literature

A relatively new career field in education has emerged in recent years -- the paraprofessional. The paraprofessional (auxiliary personnel, teacher aide) is being hired by school systems in increasing numbers to free teachers of non-professional tasks and thereby maximizing professional efficiency. The duties of paraprofessionals vary from school system to school system and indeed from class to class. According to surveys, paraprofessional duties are largely clerical in nature, but also include housekeeping and classroom management jobs (NEA, 1967). Duties of teachers and aides often overlap and it is becoming apparent that teacher aides are beginning to take on responsibility in cognitive fields (Johnson & Faunce, 1973).

Paraprofessionals now hired by school systems represent a variety of academic and socio-economic backgrounds. In some areas college experience is needed to qualify and in other areas people with limited experience are hired as a community service for on the job training (Elliot, 1972). Usually

---

[1]Based on a paper by J. S. Schumm, Florida International University, Miami, 1974.

paraprofessionals participate in some type of orientation or in-service training to prepare them for their duties, however at times this training is lacking or weak (Johnson & Faunce, 1972).

Although there is some debate about the accreditation of (Jacobson & Drije, 1972) and legal limits of (LeConte, 1973) paraprofessionals in the public school, there seems to be general satisfaction on the part of teachers and aides (Templeton, 1972). Most teachers in the country to not have aides as yet, but those who do indicate that paraprofessionals lend substantial assistance (NEA, 1967). Aides seem to have enthusiasm for their semi-professional position and are eager for the opportunity to learn new skills (Templeton, 1972). It is interesting to note that one survey indicated that teachers were anxious for school boards to hire paraprofessionals, but believed that this should not take precedence over professional salary improvement (NEA, 1967).

Although it may be years before the true effect of paraprofessional performance in the area of student achievement can be measured accurately, studies have indicated that paraprofessionals do indeed contribute to significant improvement of student achievement (Templeton, 1972; Brickell, 1971). However, the effect of paraprofessionals on student attitudes is yet uncertain and further research is needed in this area (Templeton, 1972).

In many schools, administrators and teachers recognize the contribution that paraprofessional aides make to the implementation of individualized instruction, but finances do not enable the hiring of additional staff. An increasing number of administrators, PTA's and indeed individual teachers are organizing pools of volunteer parents to aid teachers in the classroom (Hedges, 1973). Studies indicate that parent acceptance (Carroll, 1973) and parent/teacher communication (Medinnus & Johnson, 1970) have definite bearing upon the cognitive achievement of children. Indeed, according to Title I ESEA, parent participation is required in the operation of educational programs sponsored by the Title funds (Boutwell, 1971). Studies reveal that the use of parents as teacher aides results in significant student growth and achievement (Hedges, 1973).

Additional benefits of parental participation in the schools are better community relations, broadening of the school program, development of parent skills, and support for educational programs (Elliot, 1972). Perhaps the greatest disadvantages of using parents (as opposed to salaried paraprofessionals) as classroom aides are that, as in any volunteer program, parents may fail to show up and in addition it is hard to require parents to attend training sessions. However, the overall advantages of using parents in the classroom seem to outweigh these drawbacks (Hedges, 1973).

Statement of the Hypothesis

Although parent volunteers may lack the specialized training, mandatory attendance, continuity, and incentive of a salary of a paraprofessional, the parents do have a personal stake in the matter -- the achievement of their own children. What the parents may lack in training (and dependability at times) they make up in a multitude of specialized talents and enthusiasm. In addition, the enlistment of parents is much less expensive than adding additional staff members.

Considering that all of the above mentioned studies show that student achievement is improved with the presence of a salaried, trained paraprofessional or volunteer parents in the classroom, and considering the presence of a teacher aide in the classroom (either salaried or volunteer) enables professional teachers to perform with greater efficiency and improved morale, it is hypothesized that kindergarten students who have a volunteer parent pool assisting their teacher in the classroom will show comparable achievement to kindergarten students who have a salaried paraprofessional in their classroom.

REFERENCES

Boutwell, W. D. Parent Participation. PTA Magazine, 1971, 65(30), 30.

Brickell, H. M., et al. Paraprofessional influence on student achievement and attitudes and paraprofessional performance outside the classroom in district decentralized ESEA Title I and New York State Urban Education Projects in the New York City Schools. New York: Institute for Educational Development, 1971 (ERIC, ED 057 136).

Carroll, A. D. Parent acceptance, self-concept and achievement of kindergarten children (Doctoral dissertation, Auburn University, 1973). Dissertation Abstracts International, 1973, 34, 2907A-2908A. (University Microfilms No. 73-31, 616).

Elliot, D. L. Parent participation in the elementary school. Richmond, Calif.: Richmond Unified School District, 1972 (ERIC, ED 071 751).

Hedges, H. G. Extending volunteer programs in schools. St. Catharines, Niagara Centre: Ontario Institute for Studies in Education, 1973 (ERIC, ED 085 846).

Jacobson, C., & Drije, C. Role relations between professionals and paraprofessionals in Head Start. Journal of Research and Development in Education, 1972, 5(2), 95-100.

Johnson, L., & Faunce, R. W. Teacher aides: A developing role. Elementary School Journal, 1973, 74(3), 136-144.

LeConte, M. J. The legal status of paraprofessionals in education (Doctoral dissertation, Miami University, 1973). Dissertation Abstracts International, 1973, 34, 1537A. (University Microfilms No. 73-24, 492).

Medinnus, G. R., & Johnson, T. M. Parental perceptions of
        kindergarten children. The Journal of Educational Re-
        search, 1970, 63(8), 379-381.
NEA Research Division. How the profession feels about
        teacher aides. NEA Journal, 1967, 56(8), 16.
Templeton, I. Paraprofessionals: Educational management re-
        view series number 11. Eugene, Oregon: Oregon Univer-
        sity, ERIC Clearinghouse on Educational Management, 1972
        (ERIC, ED 071 145).

BEHAVIOR MODIFICATION AS AN ALTERNATIVE
TO AMPHETAMINE THERAPY IN TREATING
HYPERKINESIS IN CHILDREN[2]

INTRODUCTION

In recent years, there has been considerable public concern and controversy over the use of amphetamines in treating
hyperkinesis in children. It has been estimated that as
many as 300,000 school children are now taking these drugs
despite a lack of follow-up studies on the medication's long-
range effects (Grinspoon & Singer, 1973; Time, 1973). Diagnosis presents another problem, for even among experts there is
no consensus as to the nature of, or means for diagnosing,
what is generally referred to as the hyperkinetic impulse
disorder (Grinspoon & Singer, 1973). Most definitions, however, do agree on the major symptoms as: increased purposeless activity, impaired attention span, lack of coordination,
impulsivity, and poor powers of concentration, usually leading to disturbed behavior at home and at school (HEW, 1971).
Estimates as to the prevalence of this disorder differ according to the source. HEW estimates a 3% incidence, while
psychiatrists estimate from 4 to 10%, and some educators
estimate it as high as 15 to 20% (Grinspoon & Singer, 1973).
It has been charged that many children are given
amphetamines solely on the recommendations of school authori-
ties, and that it is sometimes far too easy for teachers to
mistake the normal restlessness of childhood for hyperkinesis
(Time, 1973). More importantly, several investigators have
found evidence of side-effects with amphetamine treatment,
including addiction, insomnia, weight loss, and headaches
(Ladd, 1971; Bosco, 1972). Others have asserted that the real
danger is not side-effects, but that drug therapy prevents
the child from learning the necessary skills of insight and
self-control (Time, 1973).
In 1971, the U. S. Department of Health, Education, and
Welfare called a conference of 15 specialists to review research and make recommendations on amphetamine treatment. In
its report, the committee emphasized the lack of adequate
longitudinal studies, and cautioned that investigation should
be made into alternative treatments, including the modification of behavior by a system of positive reinforcement (HEW,
1971). Grinspoon & Singer (1973) also see behavior modification as an emerging alternative to drug therapy, stating that
it teaches the child self-control and has a generalizing
effect to other situations. In short, various researchers
have investigated alternatives to drug therapy, with behavior
modification receiving the focus of attention as being safer,
and perhaps even more effective in the long run (Strong,
1974).

---

[2]Based on a paper by D. H. Hunt, Florida International
University, Miami, 1974.

Statement of the Problem

This study attempted to determine the comparative effectiveness of behavior modification techniques versus amphetamine therapy in reducing the symptoms of hyperkinesis in children in a classroom setting.

For purposes of definition, the techniques of behavior modification may be classified as (1) positive reinforcement, where something positive is given when acceptable behavior occurs, (2) negative reinforcement, where unacceptable behavior is followed by a negative consequence, such as isolation, and (3) techniques using both, where desirable behaviors are encouraged by positive reinforcement while undesirable ones are discouraged by negative reinforcement (Woody, 1969).

Review of Related Literature

Behavior modification procedures with respect to deviant behaviors have been subjected to numerous experimental and clinical investigations. It has been demonstrated that token reinforcement is more effective than medication in increasing adaptive behavior in retarded women (Strong, 1974). A significant decrease in hyperactive behavior among disturbed children after behavior modification therapy was reported, with carry-over into their regular school environment (Grinspoon & Singer, 1973). In a two-year experiment with a boy diagnosed as autistic, Strong (1974) demonstrated that positive reinforcement was significantly more effective than medication in reducing facial grimacing.

Besides clinical experiments, behavior modification has also been studied in school settings. Behavior modification techniques have been shown to be effective in reducing the inappropriate classroom behaviors of a ten-year-old hyperactive brain-injured boy (Woody, 1969). Another study attempted to test the effects of behavior modification in increasing task production in 24 boys rated as hyperactive by teachers (Nixon, 1969). The subjects were randomly assigned to four treatment groups, consisting of various reinforcement techniques and control. No statistically significant changes were found, although it was noted that certain children in each group made marked changes for the better. Possible sources of error, however, could have been too few treatment sessions (8), treatment groups not large enough (6 each), rater bias, since no instruments were used for evaluation, and the Hawthorne effect, since the subjects knew they were participating in a study. Finally, an interesting study by Ellis (1974) found that amphetamines had little effect on hyperactive behavior in a play setting, although it clearly affected behavior in the classroom. In conclusion, Ellis suggests that certain environmental factors might have a more potent influence on hyperactive behavior than medication. If behavior modification can be shown to be one of these factors, then perhaps an effective and safe alternative to amphetamine treatment will result.

Statement of the Hypothesis

In view of the above studies showing that the widespread use of amphetamines in treating hyperkinesis may be a dangerous practice, and reports showing behavior modification to be successful in treating a variety of behavioral disturbances, including hyperactivity, it was hypothesized that behavior modification techniques will be as effective as amphetamines in reducing the hyperactivity of children in a classroom setting.

REFERENCES

Bosco, J. The use of ritalin for treatment of minimal brain dysfunction and hyperkinesis in children, 1972 (ERIC, ED 076 540).

Burleigh, A. Development of a scale that separates hyperkinetic and normal children and demonstrates drug effect. Paper presented at the Annual Meeting of the American Educational Research Association, New York, 1971 (ERIC, ED 048 374).

Ellis, M. J. Methylphenidate and the activity of hyperactives in the informal setting. Child Development, 1974, 45, 217-220.

Grinspoon, L., & Singer, S. Amphetamines in the treatment of hyperkinetic children. Harvard Educational Review, 1973, 43, 515-555.

Health, Education and Welfare (HEW), U. S. Department of. Report of the conference on the use of stimulant drugs in the treatment of behaviorally disturbed young school children. Washington, D.C.: Author, 1971 (ERIC, ED 051 612).

Ladd, E. G. Pills for classroom peace? Education Digest, 1971, 36, 1-4.

Nixon, S. B. Increasing the frequency of attending responses in hyperactive distractible youngsters by use of operant and modeling procedures (Doctoral dissertation, Stanford University, 1965). Dissertation Abstracts, 1966, 26, 6517. (University Microfilms No. 66-025, 97).

Time, 1973, 101, 65.

Woody, R. Behavioral Problem Children in the Schools. New York: Appleton-Century-Crofts, 1969.

THE COMPARATIVE EFFECTIVENESS OF A LAB APPROACH VERSUS A TRADITIONAL APPROACH IN IMPROVING MATH COMPUTATION[3]

INTRODUCTION

Many of our students today are leaving elementary school and entering jr. high school lacking the ability to calculate with the basic operations of mathematics. The most recent standardized test scores showed that Monroe County elementary students are below the national norm in math computation. This fact, along with parent concern, has made administrators, coordinators and teachers take a hard look at the current math programs.

Many methods have been tried in an attempt to bring about an improvement in math computation skills. The latest popular aid is the use of a mathematics laboratory.

Statement of the Problem

The problem to be investigated in this study is the comparative effectiveness of a lab approach versus a traditional approach in improving the computational skill of fifth graders.

Review of Related Literature

A mathematics laboratory is an area used by students, individually or in small groups, to experiment with concepts of mathematics by using manipulative materials. These usually include items such as bulletin boards, cuisenaire rods, display cabinets, flash cards, flannel boards, manipulative puzzles, geo boards, magic squares, films, individual math kits, math records, tapes and tape recorders (Krulik, 1971; Garvey, 1972).

Lab materials are used as an extension of a regular math lesson. They can be used during part of the lesson or in a free period during the day when the students can choose what they want to do.

One advantage of the mathematics laboratory is that it lets students work on their own level with no pressure of a specific time limit (May, 1971; Rouse, 1972). A math lab is useful in providing students with more than one way of learning the same materials, and in fitting methods to the child's

---

[3]Based on a paper by C. Charette, Florida International University, Miami, 1974.

learning style (Deans, 1971; Barson, 1971). Math labs can therefore be used for motivation, enrichment or reinforcement.

A study to determine the effect of a math lab on math achievement in middle school students showed no significant difference between lab and traditional math classes (Smith, 1973). Perhaps the insufficient time allotted for use of the math lab by the experimental group affected the results. Other studies to determine the effect of manipulative materials in elementary math programs indicate that manipulative materials add reality to the learning situation (Davis, 1967), and that a math laboratory does improve interest and comprehension at the elementary level (Gray, 1973).

Statement of the Hypothesis

Considering the above-mentioned studies and the cited advantages of a math laboratory, it is hypothesized that fifth-grade students who work in a math class with a laboratory will show significantly greater computational skill than fifth-grade students in a traditional math class.

REFERENCES

Barson, A. Mathematics laboratory for elementary and middle school. The Arithmetic Teacher, 1971, 18, 565-567.

Davis, R. B. The range of rhetorics, scale, and other variables. Journal of Research and Development in Education, 1967, 1, 51-68.

Deans, E. Laboratory approach to elementary mathematics. Today's Education, 1971, 60, 20-22.

Garvey, M. Teaching Displays: Their Purpose, Construction and Use. Hamden, Conn.: Linnet Books, 1972.

Gray, T. M. A field of mathematics laboratory development in Youngstown, Ohio. Doctoral dissertation, University of Pittsburgh, 1973. University Microfilms No. 73-21, 242 (ERIC, ED 085 267).

Krulik, S., McPherson, A., & Rudnick, J. And there was no room in school! Audiovisual Instruction, 1972, 17(1), 21-22.

May, L. J. Math lab! Grade Teacher, 1971, 89, 103-105.

Rouse, W. Mathematics laboratory: Misnamed, misjudged, misunderstood. School Science and Math, 1972, 72, 48-56.

Smith, E. D. The effects of laboratory instruction upon achievement in and attitude toward mathematics of middle school students (Doctoral dissertation, Indiana University, 1973). Dissertation Abstracts International, 1974, 34, 3715A-3716A. (University Microfilms No. 74-417, 142).

3

Preparation and Evaluation of a Research Plan

TASK 3

For the hypothesis which you have
formulated, develop the remaining
components of a research plan for
a study which you would conduct in
order to test your hypothesis. Include the following:

Method
  Subjects
  Instruments
  Design
  Procedure
Data Analysis
Time Schedule

Enablers 3-1 and 3-2 involve description of the components of a research plan and ways in which research plans are
evaluated; this information is contained in Chapter 3. Task
3 entails preparation of a brief research plan. Following
this discussion, three examples are presented which illustrate the performance called for by Task 3. These examples
represent tasks submitted by the same students whose Tasks
for Chapter 2 were previously presented; consequently, the
research plans match the introductions. Keep in mind that
since you do not yet possess the necessary level of expertise,
the proposed activities described in your plan (and in the

54

examples presented) do not represent ideal research procedure. You should also be aware that research plans are usually much more detailed. The examples given, however, do represent what is expected of you at this point.

THE COMPARATIVE EFFECTIVENESS OF PARENT AIDES
VERSUS SALARIED PARAPROFESSIONALS IN
THE KINDERGARTEN CLASSROOM

METHOD

Subjects

This study will take place at three Dade County schools;
one using paraprofessional aides, one with a pool of parent-
aides, and one with no teacher aides. The schools will all
be located in an upper-middle class suburban section of the
southwest area of Dade County and each will have 3 or 4
kindergarten classes, 30 students per class. Random cluster
sampling will be used to select two classes from each of the
three schools involved.

Instrument

All students will be pretested and posttested using an
achievement test appropriate for preschool children.

Design

Six randomly selected classes will be included in this
study. All groups will be pretested and posttested.

Procedure

Two classes will be randomly selected from each of three
schools -- one school which uses paraprofessional aides, one
which uses parent aides, and one which does not utilize aides.
Although there are many terms used to refer to teacher aides
(non-professionals, auxiliary personnel, paraprofessionals)
for the sake of consistency in the study, the term paraprofessional will be used to refer to the salaried, trained group
of volunteer parents. At the beginning of the school year
all students will be pretested. Parent aides will be required to attend two training sessions, one in September and
one in January. The training sessions will be planned by
teachers and administrators of the school. The paraprofessionals will participate in an in-service training program designed by the teachers and administrators of the
school. The curriculum for the six kindergarten classes will
be standard and the groups will differ mainly with respect
to whether the teachers have an aide or not, and if they do

whether the aide is a professional or not. A limitation of this study is that the duties of teacher aides are not standardized from class to class. Depending on the professional teacher in charge, the teacher aide may have clerical, housekeeping, classroom management, or even cognitive duties. However, it is being assumed that each teacher in the study will assign duties to teacher aides which she feels will enable her to make best use of her time and training as a professional in the classroom. At the end of the school year, all the students will be posttested.

DATA ANALYSIS

The two groups within each school will be considered as a single treatment. Thus the combined performance of the two groups in each school will be compared to the combined performance of the groups in each of the other schools.

TIME SCHEDULE

Activity	Dates
Selection of subjects	August 15-30
Administration of pretest	September 15
Training of aides	September 1-15 January 15-30
Administration of posttest	June 15
Analysis of data	June 15-30
Preparation of report	Ongoing -- Completed by July 15

BEHAVIOR MODIFICATION AS AN ALTERNATIVE
TO AMPHETAMINE THERAPY IN TREATING
HYPERKINESIS IN CHILDREN

METHOD

Subjects

The sample group for this study will be selected from the population of South Side School, Carter County Center for behaviorally disturbed, elementary-age children. Only those children who have been diagnosed as "hyperkinetic" or "hyper-active" by a school psychologist will be considered as comprising the population. The method of sampling to be used will be stratified sampling, with the ages from 6 through 10 represented in the sample. Forty-five subjects will be selected, to be randomly assigned to three treatment groups.

Instrument

Pre- and posttest instruments will be the Porteus Maze Test and the Becker Child Observation System.

Design

There will be three randomly formed groups. Each group will be pretested and posttested.

Procedure

After they have been classified by age, subjects will be randomly assigned to one of three treatments. All groups will be pretested in January at the beginning of the second semester. During the second semester behavior modification techniques will be used with group 1, group 2 will receive amphetamine therapy, and group 3 will follow regular classroom procedure. Each treatment procedure will take place in a classroom setting, following the regular school hours and schedule. The facilities of South Side School will be used. Teachers of the three treatment groups will all have had a minimum of three years experience in teaching behaviorally disturbed children. The teacher of group 1 will take part in a 20-hour training session in the specific behavior modification techniques to be used. All three treatment classrooms will follow the same academic curriculum, with teachers responsible for individually programming each child.

It is assumed that all three teachers participating in the study will have the same degree of skill in individualizing instruction and programming appropriate academic tasks. It is further assumed that the individualized curriculum will prevent the age range in each classroom from being a factor influencing results.

A major limitation of the study is that results may not be generalized to populations larger than class size of 15, and to classrooms taught by teachers with no prior experience in teaching behaviorally disturbed youngsters. In May, at the end of the second semester, all subjects will be posttested.

METHOD OF ANALYSIS

The performance of the three groups will be compared using analysis of variance.

TIME SCHEDULE

	January	February	March	April	May	June
Assignment of subjects	____					
Pretesting	___					
Treatment		_____				
Posttesting					___	
Data analysis					_____	
Research report writing		_____				

THE COMPARATIVE EFFECTIVENESS OF A LAB
APPROACH VERSUS A TRADITIONAL APPROACH
IN IMPROVING MATH COMPUTATION

METHOD

Subjects

Subjects will be fifth-graders from one of Key West's elementary schools. Many of the children are military dependents.

Instrument

Students will be tested with a standardized test of computational ability.

Design

Subjects will be grouped by IQ (high, medium, low), and then 20 subjects will be selected from each IQ group. Half of each IQ group will be placed into the experimental group and half into the control group. Both groups will be pretested and posttested.

Procedure

An IQ test will be administered to all the fifth-graders and they will be classified as high, medium, or low IQ. From each IQ group 20 students will be selected. Half of the 20 students from each IQ group will be placed in the experimental group and half in the control group. The experimental group will have 30 subjects and the control group will have 30. At the beginning of the school year all students will be administered a standardized test of computational ability. For the remainder of the school year the experimental group will spend a portion of each daily math lesson in a math laboratory. The control group will also have a daily math lesson but will not participate in a math lab. The teachers selected to teach each group will be teachers with a similar number of years of experience. At the end of the school year, in June, all students will be posttested with a standardized test of computational ability.

METHOD OF ANALYSIS

The scores of the experimental and the control group will be compared using a t test.

TIME SCHEDULE

Activity	Date
Administer IQ test and group subjects by IQ	September, week 1
Form groups and administer pretest	September, week 2
Treatment	September, week 3 -- June, week 2
Administer posttest	June, week 3
Analysis	June, week 4 -- July, week 2
Write research report	October, week 1 -- August, week 2

4

Selection
of a
Sample

TASK 4

Having selected a problem, and having
formulated one or more testable hypotheses
or answerable questions, describe a sample
appropriate for evaluating your hypotheses
or answering your questions. This description will include:

a) a definition of the population from
which the sample would be drawn;
b) the procedural technique for selecting the sample and forming the groups;
c) sample sizes; and
d) possible sources of sampling bias.

Enablers 4-1 to 4-7 involve descriptions of four
sampling techniques and procedures for applying each technique. If you are going to be tested on these enablers, do
not memorize definitions. If you understand a concept you
should be able to explain it in your own words. If asked to
explain random sampling, for example, you do not have to (and
should not) quote Chapter 4 by saying "random sampling is the
process of selecting a sample in such a way that all individuals in the defined population have an equal and independent
chance of being selected for the sample." Instead, you might
say "random sampling means that every subject has the same
chance of being picked and whether or not one subject gets
picked has nothing to do with whether or not any other subject

gets picked." Your performance on Enablers 4-2, 4-4, 4-6, and 4-7 may be evaluated through a testing situation which requires you to apply a given sampling procedure to a given set of circumstances. In order to give you practice in applying each of the techniques, a number of situations follow this discussion. Three examples are given for each of the four sampling techniques. Do the first example for each technique; if your responses match the Suggested Responses you are probably ready for an enabler test and for Task 4. If you do any of the examples incorrectly, study the Suggested Response and then do the second example for that technique. If necessary, repeat the process with the third example.

ENABLER 4-2

List the procedures for using a table of random numbers to select a sample, given the following situations.

Example 1

There are 150 first graders in the population and you want a random sample of 60 students.

1. _____

_____

_____

2. _____

_____

_____

3. _____

_____

_____

4. _____

_____

_____

5. _____

_____

_____

6. _____

_____

_____

Example 2

There are 220 principals in the school system and you want a random sample of 40 principals.

1. _____

_____

_____

2. _____

_____

_____

3. _____

_____

_____

4. _____

_____

_____

5. _____

_____

_____

6. _____

_____

_____

Example 3

There are 320 students defined as gifted in the school system and you want a random sample of 50 gifted students.

1. _____

_____

_____

2. _____

_____

_____

3. _____

_____

_____

4. _____

_____

_____

5. _____

_____

_____

6. _____

_____

_____

ENABLER 4-4

List the procedures for selecting a stratified sample,
given the following situations.

Example 1

There are 500 twelfth-grade students in the population, you want a sample of 60 students, and you
want to stratify on three levels of IQ in order to
insure equal representation.

1. _____

_____

_____

2. _____

_____

_____

Example 2

There are 95 algebra I students in the population,
you want a sample of 30 students, and you want to
stratify on sex in order to insure equal representation of males and females.

1. _____

_____

_____

2. _____

_____

_____

Example 3

There are 240 principals in the school system, you
want a sample of 45 principals, and you want to
stratify by level, i.e., elementary versus secondary,
in order to insure proportional representation.
You know that there are approximately twice as
many secondary principals as elementary principals.

1. _____

    _____

    _____

2. _____

    _____

    _____

ENABLER 4-6

List the procedures for cluster sampling, given the
following situations.

Example 1

There are 80 sixth-grade classrooms in the population, each classroom has an average of 30 students,
and you want a sample of 180 students.

1. _____

    _____

    _____

2. _____

    _____

    _____

3. _____

    _____

    _____

<u>Example 2</u>

There are 75 schools in the school system, each
school has an average of 50 teachers, and you want
a sample of 350 teachers.

1. _____

_____

_____

2. _____

_____

_____

3. _____

_____

_____

<u>Example 3</u>

There are 100 kindergarten classes in the school
system, each class has an average of 20 children,
and you want a sample of 200 children.

1. _____

_____

_____

2. _____

_____

_____

3. _____

_____

_____

ENABLER 4-7

List the procedures for selecting a systematic sample, given the following situations.

Example 1

You have a list of 2000 high school students, and you want a sample of 200 students.

1. _____

_____

_____

2. _____

_____

_____

3. _____

_____

_____

Example 2

You have a directory which lists the names and addresses of 12,000 teachers and you want a sample of 2,500 teachers.

1. _____

_____

_____

2. _____

_____

_____

3. _____

_____

_____

Example 3

You have a list of 1,500 junior high school
students, and you want a sample of 100 students.

1. _____

_____

_____

2. _____

_____

_____

3. _____

_____

_____

Task 4 involves descriptions of a population and the procedure for selecting a sample from that population. Following this discussion, three examples are presented which illustrate the performance called for by Task 4. Again, these examples represent tasks submitted by the same students whose tasks for Chapters 2 and 3 were presented. Consequently, the sampling plans represent refinements of the ones included in Task 3.

THE COMPARATIVE EFFECTIVENESS OF PARENT

AIDES VERSUS SALARIED PARAPROFESSIONALS

IN THE KINDERGARTEN CLASSROOM

The sample for this investigation will be selected from all 150 children enrolled in the kindergarten at an elementary school in Hudson County. The school is located in an upper-middle class suburban area of the county. Sixty of the kindergarten children will be randomly selected (using a table of random numbers) and will then be randomly assigned (by flipping a coin) to one of two classrooms.

NOTE: Notice how this sampling plan differs from the one described for Task 3.

BEHAVIOR MODIFICATION AS AN ALTERNATIVE

TO AMPHETAMINE THERAPY IN TREATING

HYPERKINESIS IN CHILDREN

The sample group for this study will be selected from the population of South Side School, Carter County Center for behaviorally disturbed, elementary-aged children. Only those children who have been diagnosed as being "hyperkinetic" or "hyperactive" by a school psychologist will be considered as comprising the population for this study.
The population will be stratified according to age, i.e., 6, 7, 8, 9, and 10. The total sample size will be 45; 9 subjects will be randomly selected from each of the 5 age levels. Three subjects from each age level will then be randomly assigned to each of three treatment groups. Thus, each treatment group will be composed of 15 subjects, with the ages from 6 to 10 equally represented in each group.

Since the sample will be drawn from only one school, subjects may represent a rather limited population. However, the school does draw its student body from all students in Carter County.

THE COMPARATIVE EFFECTIVENESS OF A LAB

APPROACH VERSUS A TRADITIONAL APPROACH

IN IMPROVING MATH COMPUTATION

The sample for this study will be selected from 135 fifth-graders in one of Key West's elementary schools. The school has a student population of 750, and is composed primarily of military dependents. The students are mostly caucasian and Cuban-American.

The 135 fifth-grade students will be stratified according to IQ. Criterion for classification will be scores resulting from administration of the Otis-Lennon Mental Ability Test. Students will be classified as low IQ (below 90), average IQ (90-110), or high IQ (above 110). Using a table of random numbers, 20 students will be randomly selected from each of the IQ groups. Of the 20 subjects selected from each IQ group, 10 will be randomly assigned to the experimental group and 10 to the control group. Therefore, there will be two treatment groups of 30 each, stratified according to IQ.

The generalizability of the results of this study will be limited due to the narrowly defined population.

5

Selection
of
Measuring
Instruments

TASK 5

Having stated a problem, formulated one
or more hypotheses or questions, and described a sample, describe three instruments appropriate for collection of data
pertinent to the hypothesis or question.
For each instrument selected, the description will include:

a) the name, publisher and cost;
b) a description of the instrument;
c) validity and reliability data;
d) the type of subjects for whom
    the instrument is appropriate;
e) instrument administration require-
    ments;
f) training requirements for scoring;
    and
g) a synopsis of reviews.

Based on these descriptions, indicate which
test is most acceptable for your "study" and
why.

Enablers 5-1 to 5-11 involve descriptions of various types of validity and reliability and descriptions of the procedures for determining each. Enablers 5-12 to 5-19 involve descriptions of types of tests and procedures for selection and administration of tests. Again, if you are going to be tested on these enablers, do not try to memorize. Instead, see if you can explain each concept in your own words; if you can, you probably will retain the concepts much better and will be able to explain them in a testing situation. Your performance on Enablers 5-4 and 5-6 may be evaluated through a testing situation which requires you to apply a given procedure for establishing validity to a given set of circumstances. In order to give you practice in applying each of the procedures, a number of situations follow this discussion. Three examples are given for each procedure; if your responses match the Suggested Responses, you are probably ready for an enabler test. If you do either of the examples incorrectly, study the Suggested Response and then do the second example for that procedure. If necessary, repeat the procedure with the third example.

ENABLER 5-4

List procedures for determining concurrent validity, given the following situations.

Example 1

You want to determine the concurrent validity of a new IQ test for young children.

1. _____

_____

_____

2. _____

_____

_____

3. _____

_____

_____

4. _____

_____

_____

Example 2

You want to determine the concurrent validity of a new self-concept scale for junior high school students.

1. _____

_____

_____

2. _____

_____

_____

3. _____

_____

_____

4. _____

_____

_____

Example 3

You want to determine the concurrent validity of a
new reading comprehension test for high school
students.

1. _____

_____

_____

2. _____

_____

_____

3. _____

_____

_____

4. _____

_____

_____

ENABLER 5-6

List procedures for determining predictive validity,
given the following situations.

Example 1

You want to predict success in graduate school
and you want to determine the predictive validity
of the GRE.

1. _____

_____

_____

2. _____

_____

_____

3. _____

_____

_____

4. _____

_____

_____

Example 2

You want to predict level of achievement in algebra
I and you want to determine the predictive validity
of an algebra I aptitude test.

1. _____

_____

_____

2. _____

   _____

   _____

3. _____

   _____

   _____

4. _____

   _____

   _____

Example 3

You want to predict success in nursing school and you want to determine the predictive validity of a nursing aptitude test.

1. _____

   _____

   _____

2. _____

   _____

   _____

3. _____

   _____

   _____

4. _____

   _____

   _____

Task 5 involves description and comparative analysis of three measuring instruments appropriate for collection of data pertinent to your hypothesis. Since the task is relatively straightforward, only one example which illustrates the performance called for by Task 5 will be presented.

THE COMPARATIVE EFFECTIVENESS OF PARENT AIDES

VERSUS SALARIED PARAPROFESSIONALS IN

THE KINDERGARTEN CLASSROOM

Test 1 (from Buros, 7th Yearbook, #17)

a) Peabody Individual Achievement Test (PIAT)
   Lloyd M. Dunn and Frederick C. Markwardt, Jr.
   American Guidance Service, Inc.
   $24 per set of test materials and 25 record booklets
   Postage extra

b) A description -- an individual test with 1 form, with testing time of 30-40 minutes. The PIAT has five subtests
   (mathematics, reading comprehension, reading recognition,
   spelling and general information) and yields six scores
   (each of the five subtest scores plus a total).

c) Reliability: Test-retest reliabilities, based on a one-
   month interval, are presented for the total test (.82 to
   .92, median .89) and each of the subtests: mathematics
   (.52 to .84, median, .74), reading recognition (.81 to
   .94, median .88), reading comprehension (.61 to .78,
   median .64), spelling (.42 to .78, median .65), and
   general information (.70 to .88, median .76). The reading
   recognition subtest has very nearly as much reliability
   as the total test. More confidence can be placed in the
   total score than in the subtest scores. Correlations between PIAT and PPVT IQ's range from .53 to .79 with median
   .68. Validity: 7th Yearbook states no quantitative data
   on validity, however one reviewer offers the general
   statement that the PIAT "demonstrated less validity" than
   its group achievement test competitors.

d) Grades kgn -- 12

e) No formal training is required to administer the PIAT,
   however non-professional test administrators should be
   carefully instructed before using the instrument. Directions are clearly stated, but the cautions and limita-
   tions set by the authors must be carefully followed if the
   test is to be administered meaningfully.

f) No specific training requirements were mentioned.

g) PIAT is an adequate instrument for quick, generalized
   screening of achievement in the areas of mathematics,
   reading, spelling, and general information. Because it is
   designed for a wide age span, 5 subtests, and limited testing time, it is not a test for specific and comprehensive
   achievement testing. PIAT does not include subtests for
   science, social studies or study skills. Perhaps the most
   impressive feature of PIAT is its attractive format. The
   reviewers agree that PIAT has the potential for being a

well-accepted tool for quick, rough estimate of educational levels, but that more research and revision is needed for improvement in regard to its validity and subtest reliability.

Test 2 (from Buros, 7th Yearbook, #33)

a) Tests of Basic Experiences (TOBE)
   Margaret H. Moss
   McGraw-Hill
   $32.50 per 30 sets of the battery
   $9.00 per 30 copies of any one test in the battery
   $9.25 per 30 general concepts tests
   Postage extra
   $3.00 per specimen set
   Scoring service, $2.25 per battery of 4 tests
   Spanish edition available

b) A description -- a group test with 2 levels (prekindergarten -- kindergarten and kindergarten -- grade 1), one form each. TOBE is designed to test the "richness of conceptual background" of children in preschool, kindergarten, or first grade. Each of the two levels has four separate tests -- mathematics, language, science, and social studies -- and one composite test of general concepts which includes items from the other four. Each test contains 28 items and requires approximately 25 minutes to administer.

c) Reliability: No information is given in the 7th Yearbook. Validity: The procedure used to determine the content of the test is a combination of norm-referenced and criterion-referenced criteria. The manual states, "Items were selected to achieve a balance which avoided very easy and very difficult items (norm-referenced) but some items which appeared to be relatively easy or relatively difficult were retained due to the desirability of a measure of the concept inherent in the items (criterion-referenced)." In selecting the items "every attempt was made to minimize the number of items based strictly on a knowledge of factual information and to maximize the number of items based on a child's understanding of educationally relevant concepts." However, the reviewer suggests that many of the test items are not valid reflections of this data due to non-universal customs, esoteric information, and moralizing.

d) The grade level range for subjects is given as prekindergarten -- grade 1, however the manual gives no information on the age range or other characteristics of the "prekindergarten children."

e) Proctors are required to assist with the administration of this examination. Although there are no other specific administration requirements, the reviewer suggests that the teacher teach behaviors such as "mark the" and "turn

the page" in sessions prior to the administration of the
test.

f) No specific training requirements were mentioned.

g) In general the reviewer seemed pleased with the design of
TOBE and noted that the administration procedures were
very good for use with young children. The major draw-
back seems to be in the content of some test items. The
reviewer also projected widespread use of this test due
to the lack of tests for this age range for young children of widely different cultural backgrounds.

Test 3 (from Buros, 7th Yearbook, #28)

a) Stanford Early School Achievement Test (SESAT)
Richard Madden and Eric F. Gardner
Harcourt Brace Jovanovich, Inc.
$9.00 per 35 tests
$1.10 per scoring key and practice sheet
$1.50 per specimen set
scoring service, $1.50 and over per test

b) A description -- a group test with 2 levels (kindergarten-
grade 1 and grade 1.0 - 1.5), one form each. The test is
designed to appraise "the child's cognitive abilities. . .
upon entrance into kindergarten, at the end of kindergarten, or upon entrance to the first grade." The test consists of four parts: Environment, Mathematics, Letters and
Sounds, and Aural Comprehension. It yields five scores,
one for each subtest plus a total score. The testing
time is 90 minutes divided into five sessions.

c) Reliability: Split-half reliabilities range from .76 to
.85. The intercorrelations among part and total scores
range from .53 to .90. At the beginning of kindergarten
the reliabilities range from .76 for scores on Aural Comprehension to .85 for scores on Environment. The other
two subtests have reliabilities of .79. At the beginning
of grade 1, the reliabilities are .77 for Aural Comprehension, .82 for Environment and for Mathematics, and .89
for Letters and Sounds.
Validity: The manual gives no specific information regarding procedures used to determine the content of the test.
Although reviewers state that the items appear to have
both face and content validity, they felt that more
specific information should have been presented by the
authors concerning the item analysis program.

d) Form 1: kindergarten -- grade 1
Form 2: grade 1 -- grade 1.5

e) No formal training is required to administer the SESAT,
and the manual instructions are clear and specific.

f) No special training required.

g) The reviewers agree that SESAT is a well-constructed
instrument to aid teachers in determining where to begin
(what level) their instruction of the students. The test
is of moderate reliability with better than average format, directions, and item quality. The test offers good
suggestions for the teacher in using the data to design
the classroom curriculum.

From my review of the above mentioned test I have come
to the following conclusions:
1. Buros' 7th Yearbook listed very few achievement
batteries for kindergarten use. Those that were described
were not comparable in reliability and validity with achievement tests for other age levels. With the increasing emphasis on early childhood education more achievement batteries
will soon be available (according to an article I read in
the Review of Educational Research). However, after review-
ing the tests currently available, I decided to choose the
three tests mentioned above for investigation.
2. The Peabody Individual Achievement Test (PIAT) is
considered to be an exceptionally attractive test in regard
to format, however the content is designed only to determine the general level of achievement. I feel that for this
experiment, I need a more specific instrument.
3. The PIAT is an individually administered test and
I feel that it would take too much time to administer the
test to my sample. PIAT is designed for quick screening of
individual students (such as transfer students).
4. The Tests of Basic Experiences (TOBE) did not state
validity and reliability figures.
5. I was impressed with the administration procedures
for the TOBE and felt that procedure-wise it was most suited
to kindergarten children.
6. Overall, I feel that the Stanford Early School
Achievement Test is the most suited for this study. Although
the reliability is described as "average," I could not find a
test for kindergarten level with much higher reliability.
7. The Stanford test is relatively inexpensive and is
administered to a group, which would take less time from the
classroom situation.
8. According to Buros' 7th Yearbook, Stanford Achievement Tests are the "patriarch" of achievement tests. The
most "widely used over the longest period." Reviewers called
for more research in regard to the PIAT and TOBE.

6

Research Method and Procedure

TASK 6

> Having stated a problem, formulated one or
> more hypotheses, described a sample, and
> selected one or more measuring instruments,
> develop the method section of a research re-
> port. This should include a definition of
> subjects, instrument(s), research design,
> and specific procedures.

Although the Task for Chapter 6 is accompanied by many
enablers, all of the concepts related to the enablers are
discussed within the Chapter. You may be asked to complete
and submit the enablers in written form or you may be tested
on them. If a test is involved, a very good way to prepare
for it is complete the enablers as if they were going to be
submitted. This procedure will be more beneficial than simply
rereading the Chapter and will result in a good set of study
notes. It will also help if you respond to each enabler in
your own words rather than by quoting from the text. The
"buddy system" is also very effective; studying with a friend
helps to clarify fuzzy areas (two heads are better than one)
and to solidify all learned concepts.

Task 6 involves development of the method section of
your research report. The examples which follow were prepared by the same students who prepared previous examples and
you therefore should be able to see how Task 6 builds on previous Tasks. Keep in mind that Tasks 3, 4 and 5 will not

appear in your final research report; Task 6 will. Therefore, each of the important points in those previous tasks
should be included in Task 6. Since earlier it was recom-
mended that you design an experimental study, the three examples all represent experimental research. If your study
represents one of the other methods of research, you should
be able to generalize from the following examples.

THE COMPARATIVE EFFECTIVENESS OF PARENT AIDES
VERSUS SALARIED PARAPROFESSIONALS IN
THE KINDERGARTEN CLASSROOM

METHOD

Description of Subjects

The sample for this investigation was selected from all 120 children enrolled in the kindergarten level at an elementary school in Hudson County. This school is located in the upper-middle class, suburban southwest area of the County. Sixty of the kindergarten children were randomly selected (using a table of random numbers) and were then randomly assigned to one of the two classrooms participating in this nine-month study.

Description of Instrument

The Stanford Early School Achievement Test (SESAT) -- Level 1 was selected and used as the data gathering instrument for this study. Although the reliability and validity for this battery were described as "average," it did compare favorably with other achievement tests now available for the kindergarten level. The format, directions for administration, and price also compared positively with other early childhood achievement batteries. The SESAT consists of four parts (Environment, Mathematics, Letters and Sounds, and Aural Comprehension) and yields five scores, one for each subtest plus a total score. The testing time is 90 minutes, divided into 5 sessions. In general, the SESAT meets the demands of an instrument of measurement for this investigation in that it is a group administered test which is designed to appraise cognitive abilities of children upon entrance into and/or completion of kindergarten.

Description of Experimental Design

The design used in this study was the pretest-posttest control group design (See Figure 1).

This design was selected because of the feasibility of randomization, the need to check for initial equivalency of the two groups, and the desire to obtain information on the cognitive abilities of each child at the beginning of the study. While this design controls quite well for sources of internal invalidity, external validity may be weakened due to pretest-treatment interaction. This potential problem, however, was believed to be minimized in this study because of the age and naivete of the subjects and the duration of the study (nine months).

87

		PRETEST	TREATMENT	POSTTEST
GROUP A				
Parent-Aide n=30 (15 from CLASS 1 and 15 from CLASS 2)	RANDOM ASSIGNMENT	Stanford Early School Achievement Test	Regular Instructional Program Plus Parent-Aide	Stanford Early School Achievement Test
GROUP B				
Paraprofessional Aide n=30 (15 from CLASS 1 and 15 from CLASS 2)	RANDOM ASSIGNMENT	Stanford Early School Achievement Test	Regular Instructional Program Plus Paraprofessional Aide	Stanford Early School Achievement Test

Figure 1. Experimental design.

Procedure

The 60 randomly selected students were randomly assigned to one of two classes, Class 1 or Class 2. After being assigned to a class, the students were randomly placed in one of the two experimental groups by tossing a coin. Therefore, the organization of this study was:

GROUP 1-A   Teacher 1, Treatment A
                       (parent aide) (n = 15)
GROUP 1-B   Teacher 1, Treatment B
                       (paraprofessional aide) (n = 15)
GROUP 2-A   Teacher 2, Treatment A
                       (parent aide) (n = 15)
GROUP 2-B   Teacher 2, Treatment B
                       (paraprofessional aide) (n = 15)

The two teachers involved in the study each had more than five years teaching experience and had recently participated in a workshop on individualized instruction sponsored by the school. The established program for instruction was not altered. The classroom teachers carried out programs in the usual manner.

Parent-aide pools were organized by the administration. Five parent aides (one scheduled for each morning of the week) plus two on-call alternates were assigned to Class 1 and Class 2. Parents were asked to be on duty between 9 a.m. and 12 p.m. on their assigned day. Parents were also required to attend training sessions held in September and January. The sessions were planned by the administrators and teachers in cooperation with the researcher. Paraprofessional aides were hired for both Class 1 and Class 2. The paraprofessional aides worked five days a week from 9 a.m. - 12 p.m. All aides participated in an inservice training program organized by the administrator and teachers in cooperation with the researcher.

At the beginning of the school year, the Stanford Early School Achievement Test was administered to all subjects. The tests were conducted in the individual classrooms. All scores were recorded on file cards and stored.

Duties of the parent aides and paraprofessional aides were identical. The aides were assigned to work with 1-5 children at a time -- the assignment being determined by teacher evaluation of student needs. Responsibilities included grading papers, assisting absentees with make-up work, aiding with enrichment activities for advanced students and aiding in remedial instruction as needed. Specific instructions were given by the teacher in all cases. The only restriction was that the aide was to stay within the limits of his (her) assigned group of students (even in regard to grading papers).

At the end of the school year, the Stanford Early School Achievement Test was again administered in an identical manner to both classes. The results were tabulated and recorded.

BEHAVIOR MODIFICATION AS AN ALTERNATIVE TO
AMPHETAMINE THERAPY IN TREATING
HYPERKINESIS IN CHILDREN

METHOD

Description of Subjects

The sample group for this study was selected from the population of South Side School, a center for behaviorally disturbed youngsters which draws its student body from all elementary schools in Carter County. All children in the sample group had been diagnosed as being "hyperkinetic" or "hyperactive" by a school psychologist prior to their placement at South Side. Forty-five subjects comprised the sample group, which was stratified according to age, with the age levels from six through ten equally represented.

Description of Instrument

The pretest and posttest instrument selected was the Porteus Maze Test, which has been shown in various studies to be a valid and reliable measure of impulsivity and the ability to sustain attention and concentration. It has also been shown to be a reliable indicator of drug effect, discriminating between those hyperactive children on medication and those not taking drugs (Burleigh, 1971). Thus, this instrument was selected to measure three factors of the definition of hyperkinesis: impulsivity, impaired attention span, and poor powers of concentration.

Research Design

The design utilized in this study was the pretest, posttest, control group design (see Figure 1). Three treatment groups were formed: Group 1, behavior modification techniques; Group 2, amphetamine treatment; and Group 3, control, to use regular classroom procedures. This design was chosen because it was considered essential to obtain a pre-treatment measure of hyperactivity in order to reliably evaluate the effects of the treatments. And, since five months elapsed between pre- and posttesting, possible interaction of testing and treatment was not considered to be a major threat to the external validity of the study.

Groups		Pretest	Treatment	Posttest
Group 1 n = 15	R	Porteus Maze Test	Behavior Modification	Porteus Maze Test
Group 2 n = 15	R	Porteus Maze Test	Amphetamine therapy	Porteus Maze Test
Group 3 n = 15	R	Porteus Maze Test	Usual class-room proce-dures	Porteus Maze Test

Figure 1. The experimental design.

Procedure

Nine subjects were randomly selected from each of the five age groups 6, 7, 8, 9, and 10, using a table of random numbers. Then, three subjects from each age group were randomly assigned into one of the treatment groups. Thus, each treatment group comprised 15 subjects, with the ages 6 through 10 equally represented.

After the subjects were selected, they were administered the Porteus Maze Test as a pre-treatment measure of hyperactivity. Three vacant classrooms at South Side School were set up and utilized as the setting for the treatment procedures. Regular school schedule and hours were observed. Treatment conditions began on January 13, 1974.

Teachers of the groups all had had at least three years experience in teaching behaviorally disturbed children. The teacher of Group 1 took part in a 20-hour training session in the specific behavior modification techniques that were to be used. All three treatment classrooms followed the same academic curriculum, with the teachers individually programming each child. The treatments were as follows:

Group 1, behavior modification: The check-card system was employed, with each child receiving check marks for completion of academic tasks, in-seat behavior, working quietly, and other appropriate classroom behaviors. The system was organized so that each child could earn up to 100 checks per day. Earned checks were traded in at the end of each day for tangible prizes which included candy, comic books, and small toys. Inappropriate behavior was ignored unless it endangered the child or others, in which case the time-out procedure was used (the child was removed to a small, bare, adjacent room for a specified period of time, not to exceed ten minutes).

91

Group 2, amphetamine treatment: The physician assigned to South Side School examined each child in Group 2 and prescribed an appropriate dosage of medication. The physician was available for the duration of the study to follow up and revise dosages as necessary.

Group 3, the control group: Regular classroom management procedures and techniques were followed.

On May 19, 1974, the Porteus Maze Test was re-administered to all subjects, as a post-treatment measure of hyperactivity level.

THE COMPARATIVE EFFECTIVENESS OF A LAB
APPROACH VERSUS A TRADITIONAL APPROACH IN
IMPROVING MATH COMPUTATION

METHOD

Description of Subjects

The sample for this study was selected from all fifth graders in one of Key West's elementary schools. The school has a student population of 750, and is composed primarily of military dependents. The students are mostly caucasian and Cuban-American.

Description of Instrument

The instrument used to test the students was the Stanford Achievement Test: Arithmetic Test. This test has been found to be reliable, with reported reliabilities in the range .86 to .93, and measures students' computational ability.

Description of Experimental Design

The design chosen for this study was the pretest-posttest control group design (See Figure 1).

	Pretest	Treatment	Posttest
R Experimental n = 30	SAT: AT*	Mathematics Laboratory	SAT: AT*
R Control n = 30	SAT: AT*	Traditional Classroom	SAT: AT*

*Stanford Achievement Test: Arithmetic Test

Figure 1. Experimental design.

This design was selected because of the controls which it provides for sources of invalidity. The only major threat to validity associated with design is possible pretest-treatment interaction, which may limit generalizability. This potential threat was assumed to be minimized in this study, however, because of the nonreactive nature of the pretest and the fact that there was an interval of eight months between pretesting and posttesting.

Procedure

The 135 fifth-grade students were stratified according to IQ. The criterion for classification was scores resulting from administration of the Otis-Lennon Mental Ability Test. Students were classified as low IQ (below 90), average IQ (90-110), or high IQ (above 110). Using a table of random numbers, 20 students were randomly selected from each IQ group. Of the 20 subjects selected from each IQ group, 10 were randomly assigned to the experimental group and 10 to the control group. Thus, there were two treatment groups of 30 subjects each, stratified according to IQ.

Both classes took the Stanford Achievement Test: Arithmetic Test in September. The control group spent the next 8 months in a traditional classroom, while the experimental group had a math lab which was used as part of the daily math lesson. The lab encompassed various manipulative materials. Both groups used the Holt, Rinehart Math Series and the two teachers involved both had more than three years of teaching experience.

In May the Stanford Achievement Test: Arithmetic Test was again administered as a posttest to both classes.

7

Data Analysis
and
Interpretation

TASK 7

Based on Tasks 2-6 which you have already
completed, write the results section of a
research report. Generate data for each of
the subjects in your study, summarize and
describe the data using descriptive statistics, statistically analyze the data using
inferential statistics, and interpret the
results in terms of your original research
hypothesis. Present the results of your
data analyses in a summary table.

Enablers 7-1 to 7-11, 7-13 to 7-31, and 7-33 to 7-40
all involve concepts related to the organization, analysis,
and interpretation of data. Again, if you are going to be
tested on these concepts, study with a friend and make sure
you can explain each concept in your own words. Enablers
7-12 and 7-32 involve the computation and interpretation of
various descriptive and inferential statistics. In order to
give you practice in calculating the various statistics, one
more example of each statistic which you are responsible for
has been worked out for you. Perform the required operations
yourself before checking the Suggested Responses. Double
check all your figures. Students rarely have trouble with
the statistical formulas; it is usually the arithmetic that
hangs them up.

SELF-TEST FOR ENABLERS 7-12 AND 7-32

ENABLER 7-12

X
2
4
4
5
6
6
6
7
8
9

$\overline{X}$ =

SD =

X	Y
2	6
4	6
4	7
5	8
6	9

$\underline{r}$ =

$\underline{z}_1 =$

$\underline{z}_2 =$

$\underline{z}_3 =$

$\underline{z}_4 =$

$\underline{z}_5 =$

$\underline{z}_6 =$

$\underline{z}_7 =$

$\underline{z}_8 =$

$\underline{z}_9 =$

$\underline{z}_{10} =$

X_1	X_2	X_3
2	3	7
3	3	8
4	4	8
5	5	8
7	6	9

---

t test for independent samples (p = .05)

WORK SPACE

$\underline{t}$ test for nonindependent samples ($\underline{p}$ = .05)

Simple analysis of variance for 3 groups   ($\underline{p}$ = .05)

WORK SPACE

Duncan's new multiple range test (p = .01)

Chi Square -- χ^2 (p = .05)

Task 7 involves computation and interpretation of the descriptive and inferential statistics which are appropriate given your research hypothesis. The examples which follow were developed by the same students who prepared the previous examples. Do not forget that while the examples represent the performance required by Task 7, you must also submit the calculations involved in arriving at the figures which you will present in table form.

THE COMPARATIVE EFFECTIVENESS OF PARENT AIDES VERSUS SALARIED PARAPROFESSIONALS IN THE KINDERGARTEN CLASSROOM

RESULTS

The Stanford Early School Achievement Test (Level 1) was administered as a pretest to both the parent and paraprofessional groups. Examination of the means indicated that the groups were essentially equivalent on the pretest measure at the beginning of the study (See Table 1). Treatment was administered to both groups during the nine-month school year and at the end of this period the Stanford Early School Achievement Test (Level 1) was administered again to both groups. A t test for independent samples was used to compare the achievement of the two groups. This statistical technique was employed because the groups were independent of each other, i.e., subjects were randomly assigned to either the parent group or the paraprofessional group. It was found that the two groups did not differ significantly (See Table 1).

Therefore, the original hypothesis that "kindergarten students who have a volunteer parent pool assisting their teacher in the classroom will show comparable achievement to kindergarten students who have a salaried paraprofessional in their classroom" was supported.

Table 1

Means, Standard Deviations, and t for the
Parent Group and the Paraprofessional
Group on the Pretest and Posttest

Test	Group		t
	Parent	Paraprofessional	
Pretest			
Mean	51.15	50.40	
SD	14.33	13.56	
Posttest			
Mean	72.21	70.47	.51*
SD	15.06	14.42	

*$\underline{df}$ = 58, $\underline{p}$ > .05

107

BEHAVIOR MODIFICATION AS AN ALTERNATIVE
TO AMPHETAMINE THERAPY IN TREATING
HYPERKINESIS IN CHILDREN

RESULTS

Examination of pretest means indicated that the groups were essentially the same at the beginning of the study (See Table 1). Porteus Maze scores range from 0-20, with higher scores indicating higher levels of impulsivity and less ability to sustain attention. As Table 1 indicates, levels of hyperactivity were quite high in all three groups, with mean scores of 14.7, 14.9, and 15.2 respectively.

Table 1

Means and Standard Deviations for the Behavior
Modification, Amphetamine Therapy, and Control
Groups on the Pretest and Posttest

| | Group | | |
	Behavior Modification[*]	Amphetamine Therapy[*]	Control[*]
Pretest			
Mean	14.7	14.9	15.2
SD	3.1	2.7	2.8
Posttest			
Mean	6.8	6.7	14.8
SD	1.8	1.7	2.6

[*] n = 15

Following the five-month treatment period, the Porteus Maze Test was again administered to all subjects. The post-test scores of the three randomly formed groups were compared using a one-way analysis of variance. It was found that the groups differed significantly (F = 66.13, $\underline{df}$ = 2/42, $\underline{p}$ < .05). Application of Duncan's new multiple range test with $\underline{p}$ = .01 revealed that while the behavior modification and amphetamine therapy groups did not differ significantly (6.8 versus 6.7), both treatment groups did differ significantly from the control group (6.8 versus 14.8 and 6.7 versus 14.8). The

control group maintained essentially the same level of hyperactivity during the five-month period (15.2 versus 14.8); the
level of hyperactivity was reduced in both experimental
groups, from 14.7 to 6.8 and from 14.9 to 6.7 (See Table 1).
Thus, the original hypothesis that "behavior modification
techniques will be as effective as amphetamines in reducing
the hyperactivity of children in a classroom setting" was
supported.

THE COMPARATIVE EFFECTIVENESS OF A LAB
APPROACH VERSUS A TRADITIONAL APPROACH
IN IMPROVING MATH COMPUTATION

The Stanford Achievement Test: Arithmetic Test was administered to both the experimental and control groups as a pretest. Inspection of the means indicated that as a result of random assignment the groups were basically the same on initial computational skill (See Table 1). Eight months later, the Stanford Achievement Test: Arithmetic Test was administered to both groups as a posttest. A t test for independent samples was used to compare the two groups on the posttest results. It was found that the groups differed significantly (See Table 1).

Table 1

Means, Standard Deviations, and t for the
Experimental and Control Groups on the
Pretest and Posttest

Test	Group		t
	Experimental	Control	
Pretest			
Mean	50.04	48.20	
SD	14.14	14.31	
Posttest			
Mean	60.27	75.82	3.54*
SD	10.11	8.97	

*$\underline{df}$ = 58, $\underline{p}$ < .05

Therefore, the original hypothesis that "fifth-grade students who work in a math lab class with a laboratory will show significantly greater computational skill than fifth-grade students in a traditional math class" was supported.

Preparation
of a
Research
Report

TASK 8

> Based on Tasks 2, 6 and 7, prepare a
> research report which follows the general
> format for a thesis or dissertation.

Enablers 8-1 and 8-4 involve descriptions of guidelines
for preparing various types of research reports; this information is contained in Chapter 8. Task 8 entails combining
Tasks 2, 6 and 7, preparing preliminary pages, and adding
sections for conclusions and recommendations and a summary.
Since Task 8 is relatively straightforward, only one example
which illustrates the performance called for will be presented. This example represents the synthesis of the previously
presented Tasks related to alternate methods of treating
hyperkinetic children.

BEHAVIOR MODIFICATION AS AN ALTERNATIVE

TO AMPHETAMINE THERAPY IN TREATING

HYPERKINESIS IN CHILDREN

Dayna Hunt

TASK 8

Submitted in partial fulfillment of
the requirements for EDU 507
Florida International University
July, 1974

TABLE OF CONTENTS

---

[1]Example page numbers are in parentheses in order to differentiate them from the page numbers of this book.

LIST OF TABLES

(ii)

LIST OF FIGURES

INTRODUCTION

In recent years, there has been considerable public concern and controversy over the use of amphetamines in treating
hyperkinesis in children. It has been estimated that as many
as 300,000 school children are now taking these drugs despite
a lack of follow-up studies on the medication's long-range
effects (Grinspoon & Singer, 1973; Time, 1973). Diagnosis
presents another problem, for even among experts there is no
consensus as to the nature of, or means for diagnosing, what
is generally referred to as the hyperkinetic impulse disorder
(Grinspoon & Singer, 1973). Most definitions, however, do
agree on the major symptoms as: increased purposeless activity, impaired attention span, lack of coordination, impulsivity, and poor powers of concentration, usually leading to disturbed behavior at home and at school (HEW, 1971). Estimates
as to the prevalence of this disorder differ according to
the source. HEW estimates a 3% incidence, while psychiatrists
estimate from 4 to 10%, and some educators estimate it as high
as 15 to 20% (Grinspoon & Singer, 1973).
It has been charged that many children are given
amphetamines solely on the recommendations of school authori-
ties, and that it is sometimes far too easy for teachers to
mistake the normal restlessness of childhood for hyperkinesis
(Time, 1973). More importantly, several investigators have
found evidence of side-effects with amphetamine treatment,
including addiction, insomnia, weight loss, and headaches
(Ladd, 1971; Bosco, 1972). Others have asserted that the
real danger is not side-effects, but that drug therapy prevents the child from learning the necessary skills of insight
and self-control (Time, 1973).
In 1971, the U.S. Department of Health, Education, and
Welfare called a conference of 15 specialists to review research and make recommendations on amphetamine treatment. In
its report, the committee emphasized the lack of adequate
longitudinal studies, and cautioned that investigation should
be made into alternative treatments, including the modification of behavior by a system of positive reinforcement (HEW,
1971). Grinspoon & Singer (1973) also see behavior modification as an emerging alternative to drug therapy, stating that
it teaches the child self-control and has a generalizing
effect to other situations. In short, various researchers
have investigated alternatives to drug therapy, with behavior
modification receiving the focus of attention as being safer,
and perhaps even more effective in the long run (Strong,
1974).

Statement of the Problem

This study attempted to determine the comparative effectiveness of behavior modification techniques versus ampheta-

(1)

mine therapy in reducing the symptoms of hyperkinesis in children in a classroom setting.

For purposes of definition, the techniques of behavior modification may be classified as (1) positive reinforcement, where something positive is given when acceptable behavior occurs, but is withheld when unacceptable behavior occurs, (2) negative reinforcement, where unacceptable behavior is followed by a negative consequence, such as isolation, and (3) techniques using both, where desirable behaviors are encouraged by positive reinforcement while undesirable ones are discouraged by negative reinforcement (Woody, 1969).

Review of Related Literature

Behavior modification procedures with respect to deviant behaviors have been subjected to numerous experimental and clinical investigations. It has been demonstrated that token reinforcement is more effective than medication in increasing adaptive behavior in retarded women (Strong, 1974). A significant decrease in hyperactive behavior among disturbed children after behavior modification therapy was reported, with carry-over into their regular school environment (Grinspoon & Singer, 1973). In a two-year experiment with a boy diagnosed as autistic, Strong (1974) demonstrated that positive reinforcement was significantly more effective than medication in reducing facial grimacing.

Besides clinical experiments, behavior modification has also been studied in school settings. Behavior modification techniques have been shown to be effective in reducing the inappropriate classroom behaviors of a ten-year-old hyperactive brain-injured boy (Woody, 1969). Another study attempted to test the effects of behavior modification in increasing task production in 24 boys rated as hyperactive by teachers (Nixon, 1969). The subjects were randomly assigned to four treatment groups, consisting of various reinforcement techniques and control. No statistically significant changes were found, although it was noted that certain children in each group made marked changes for the better. Possible sources of error, however, could have been too few treatment sessions (8), treatment groups not large enough (6 each), rater bias, since no instruments were used for evaluation, and the Hawthorne effect, since the subjects knew they were participating in a study. Finally, an interesting study by Ellis (1974) found that amphetamines had little effect on hyperactive behavior in a play setting, although it clearly affected behavior in the classroom. In conclusion, Ellis suggests that certain environmental factors might have a more potent influence on hyperactive behavior than medication. If behavior modification can be shown to be one of these factors, then perhaps an effective and safe alternative to amphetamine treatment will result.

(2)

Statement of the Hypothesis

In view of the above studies showing that the widespread
use of amphetamines in treating hyperkinesis may be a dangerous practice, and reports showing behavior modification to be
successful in treating a variety of behavioral disturbances,
including hyperactivity, it was hypothesized that behavior
modification techniques will be as effective as amphetamines
in reducing the hyperactivity of children in a classroom setting.

(3)

METHOD

Description of Subjects

The sample group for this study was selected from the population of South Side School, a center for behaviorally disturbed youngsters which draws its student body from all elementary schools in Carter County. All children in the sample group had been diagnosed as being "hyperkinetic" or "hyperactive" by a school psychologist prior to their placement at South Side. Forty-five subjects comprised the sample group, which was stratified according to age, with the age levels from 6 through 10 equally represented.

Description of Instrument

The pretest and posttest instrument selected was the Porteus Maze Test, which has been shown in various studies to be a valid and reliable measure of impulsivity and the ability to sustain attention and concentration. It has also been shown to be a reliable indicator of drug effect, discriminating between those hyperactive children on medication and those not taking drugs (Burleigh, 1971). Thus, this instrument was selected to measure three factors of the definition of hyperkinesis; impulsivity, impaired attention span, and poor power of concentration.

Research Design

The design utilized in this study was the pretest, posttest, control group design (See Figure 1). Three treatment groups were formed: Group 1, behavior modification techniques; Group 2, amphetamine treatment; and Group 3, control, to use regular classroom procedures. This design was chosen because it was considered essential to obtain a pre-treatment measure of hyperactivity in order to reliably evaluate the effects of the treatments. And, since five months elapsed between pre- and posttesting, possible interaction of testing and treatment was not considered to be a major threat to the external validity of the study.

Procedure

Nine subjects were randomly selected from each of the five age groups 6, 7, 8, 9, and 10, using a table of random numbers. Then, three subjects from each age group were randomly assigned into one of the treatment groups. Thus, each treatment group comprised 15 subjects, with the ages 6 through 10 equally represented.

(4)

Groups	Pretest	Treatment	Posttest
Group 1 n = 15 R	Porteus Maze Test	Behavior Modification	Porteus Maze Test
Group 2 n = 15 R	Porteus Maze Test	Amphetamine Therapy	Porteus Maze Test
Group 3 n = 15 R	Porteus Maze Test	Usual classroom procedures	Porteus Maze Test

Figure 1. The experimental design.

After the subjects were selected, they were administered the Porteus Maze Test as a pre-treatment measure of hyperactivity. Three vacant classrooms at South Side School were set up and utilized as the setting for the treatment procedures. Regular school schedule and hours were observed. Treatment conditions began on January 13, 1974.

Teachers of the groups all had had at least three years experience in teaching behaviorally disturbed children. The teacher of Group 1 took part in a 20-hour training session in the specific behavior modification techniques that were to be used. All three treatment classrooms followed the same academic curriculum, with the teachers individually programming each child. The treatments were as follows:

Group 1, behavior modification: The check-card system was employed, with each child receiving check marks for completion of academic tasks, in-seat behavior, working quietly, and other appropriate classroom behaviors. The system was organized so that each child could earn up to 100 checks per day. Earned checks were traded in at the end of each day for tangible prizes which included candy, comic books, and small toys. Inappropriate behavior was ignored unless it endangered the child or others, in which case the time-out procedure was used (the child was removed to a small, bare, adjacent room for a specified period of time, not to exceed ten minutes).

Group 2, amphetamine treatment: The physician assigned to South Side School examined each child in Group 2 and prescribed an appropriate dosage of medication. The physician was available for the duration of the study to follow up and revise dosages as necessary.

(5)

Group 3, the control group: Regular classroom
management procedures and techniques were followed.

On May 19, 1974, the Porteus Maze Test was re-administered to all subjects, as a post-treatment measure of hyperactivity level.

Examination of pretest means indicated that the groups were essentially the same at the beginning of the study (See Table 1). Porteus Maze scores range from 0-20, with higher scores indicating higher levels of impulsivity and less ability to sustain attention. As Table 1 indicates, levels of hyperactivity were quite high in all three groups, with mean scores of 14.7, 14.9, and 15.2 respectively.

Table 1

Means and Standard Deviations for the Behavior
Modification, Amphetamine Therapy, and Control
Groups on the Pretest and Posttest

| | Group | | |
	Behavior Modification[*]	Amphetamine Therapy	Control[*]
Pretest			
Mean	14.7	14.9	15.2
SD	3.1	2.7	2.8
Posttest			
Mean	6.8	6.7	14.8
SD	1.8	1.7	2.6

[*]$n = 15$

Following the five-month treatment period, the Porteus Maze Test was again administered to all subjects. The posttest scores of the three randomly formed groups were compared using a one-way analysis of variance. It was found that the groups differed significantly ($F = 66.13$, $df = 2/42$, $p < .05$). Application of Duncan's new multiple range test with $p = .01$ revealed that while the behavior modification and amphetamine therapy groups did not differ significantly (6.8 versus 6.7) both treatment groups did differ significantly from the control group (6.8 versus 14.8 and 6.7 versus 14.8). The control group maintained essentially the same level of hyperactivity during the five-month period (15.2 versus 14.8); the level of hyperactivity was reduced in both experimental groups, from 14.7 to 6.8 and from 14.9 to 6.7 (See Table 1). Thus, the original hypothesis that "behavior modification techniques will be as effective as amphetamines in reducing the hyperactivity of children in a classroom setting" was supported.

(7)

CONCLUSIONS AND RECOMMENDATIONS

Based on the above results, it was concluded that behavior modification techniques and amphetamine treatment were
equally effective in reducing hyperactivity in elementary-aged
children. Thus, the original hypothesis, that behavior modification would be as effective as medication in treating
these youngsters, was supported. Since this study utilized
classroom groups of 15, and teachers who had prior experience
in handling behaviorally disturbed children, results cannot
be generalized to regular classroom situations. However, in
view of the results, it would appear that research investiga-
ting the feasibility of using behavior modification techniques
with larger groups of hyperactive children, and with regular
elementary teachers, is warranted. If regular teachers could
be trained to recognize and modify some of the behavioral
symptoms of hyperkinesis, perhaps the widespread and cursory
use of amphetamine drugs with these children could be curtail-
ed and minimized.

(8)

SUMMARY

The purpose of this study was to determine whether application of behavior modification techniques can be an effective and safe alternative to amphetamine therapy in treating hyperkinesis in children. By using a pretest-posttest control group design, a one-way analysis of variance, and Duncan's new multiple range test, it was found that after a five-month period behavior modification was equally effective as amphetamine therapy in reducing levels of hyperactivity. It was concluded that further research is needed to determine the generalizability of the finding to larger groups and to non-special education classes.

(9)

REFERENCES

Bosco, J. The use of ritalin for treatment of minimal brain dysfunction and hyperkinesis in children, 1972 (ERIC, ED 076 540).

Burleigh, A. Development of a scale that separates hyperkinetic and normal children and demonstrates drug effect. Paper presented at the Annual Meeting of the American Educational Research Association, New York, 1971 (ERIC ED 048 374).

Ellis, M. J. Methylphenidate and the activity of hyperactives in the informal setting. Child Development, 1974, 45, 217-220.

Grinspoon, L., & Singer, S. Amphetamines in the treatment of hyperkinetic children. Harvard Educational Review, 1973, 43, 515-555.

Health, Education and Welfare (HEW), U. S. Department of. Report of the conference on the use of stimulant drugs in the treatment of behaviorally disturbed young school children. Washington, D. C.: Author, 1971 (ERIC ED 051 612).

Ladd, E. G. Pills for classroom peace? Education Digest, 1971, 36, 1-4.

Nixon, S. Increasing the frequency of attending responses in hyperactive distractible youngsters by use of operant and modeling procedures (Doctoral dissertation, Stanford University, 1965). Dissertation Abstracts, 1966, 26, 6517. (University Microfilms No. 66-025, 97).

Time, 1973, 101, 65.

Woody, R. Behavioral Problem Children in the Schools. New York: Appleton-Century-Crofts, 1969.

(10)

Evaluation of a Research Report

TASK 9

> Given a reprint of a research report and
> an evaluation form, evaluate the compo-
> nents of the report.

Enablers 9-1 and 9-2 involve identification of evaluative
questions which should be asked in order to determine the
adequacy of a research study. Task 9 entails application of
those questions to the evaluation of an actual research report. In order to give you practice in evaluating a research
study, one of the reports presented in Chapter 1, Immediate
Knowledge of Results and Test Performance, has been evaluated
for you. The SELF-TEST FOR TASK 9 which follows shortly lists
questions for you to answer with respect to that article. In
answering the questions, use the following codes:

    Y = Yes
    N = No
    ? = Cannot tell (it cannot be determined from the
        information given)
    O = Not mentioned in the article
   NA = Question not applicable
    X = Given your current level of competence, you are not
        in a position to make a judgment.

When appropriate, as you answer the questions, underline
components which correspond to questions to which you have
responded "Y". For example, if you decide that there is a

statement of the problem, underline it in the article. Since
the study which you are going to evaluate is experimental,
you are also asked to identify and diagram the experimental
design used. If your responses match reasonably well with
those given in the Suggested Responses, you are probably
ready for Task 9. Make sure that you understand the reason
for any discrepancies, especially on questions for which
responses are less judgmental and more objective; adequacy
of the literature review is more judgmental whereas the
presence or absence of a hypothesis can be objectively determined.

Immediate Knowledge of Results and Test
Performance

GENERAL EVALUATION CRITERIA

Introduction

Problem   CODE

    Is there a statement of the problem?   _____
    Is the problem "researchable"?   _____
    Is background information on the problem
        presented?   _____
    Is the educational significance of the
        problem discussed?   _____
    Does the problem statement indicate the
        variables of interest and the specific
        relationship between those variables
        which was investigated?   _____
    When necessary, are variables directly
        or operationally defined?   _____

Review of Related Literature

    Is the review comprehensive?   _____
    Are all references cited relevant to
        the problem under investigation?   _____
    Are the sources mostly primary or were
        a number of secondary sources cited?   _____
    Have references been critically analyzed
        and the results of various studies
        compared and contrasted or is the
        review basically a series of ab-
        stracts or annotations?   _____
    Is the review well-organized, does it
        logically flow in such a way that
        the references least related to the
        problem are discussed first and the
        most related references are dis-
        cussed last?   _____
    Does the review conclude with a brief
        summary of the literature and its
        implications for the problem investi-
        gated?   _____
    Do the implications discussed form an
        empirical or theoretical rationale
        for the hypotheses which follow?   _____

Hypotheses

Are specific questions to be answered listed or specific hypotheses to be tested stated? _____

Does each hypothesis state an expected relationship or difference between two variables? _____

If necessary, are variables directly or operationally defined? _____

Is each hypothesis testable? _____

Method

Subjects

Are the size and major characteristics of the population studied described? _____

Was the entire population studied? _____

Was a sample selected? _____

Is the method of selecting a sample clearly described? _____

Is the method of sample selection described one that is likely to result in a representative, unbiased sample? _____

Were volunteers used? _____

Are the size and major characteristics of the sample described? _____

Does the sample size meet the suggested guideline for minimum sample size appropriate for the method of research represented? _____

Instruments

Is a rationale given for selection of the instruments used? _____

Is each instrument described in terms of purpose and content? _____

Are the instruments appropriate for measuring the intended variables? _____

If an instrument was developed specifically for the study, are the procedures involved in its development and validation described? _____

Is evidence presented that indicates that each instrument is appropriate for the sample under study? _____

Is instrument validity discussed and
   coefficients given if appropriate?   _____
Is reliability discussed in terms of type
   and size of reliability coefficients? _____
If appropriate, are subtest reliabilities
   given?   _____
If an instrument was specifically developed
   for the study, are administration,
   scoring, and interpretation procedures
   fully described?   _____

Design and Procedure

Is the design appropriate for testing the
   hypotheses of the study?   _____
Are procedures described in sufficient
   detail to permit them to be replicated
   by another researcher?   _____
Was a pilot study conducted?   _____
If a pilot study was conducted are its
   execution and results described, as
   well as its impact on the subsequent
   study?   _____
Are control procedures described?   _____
Are there any potentially confounding
   variables which were not controlled?   _____

Results

Are appropriate descriptive statistics
   presented?   _____
Was the probability level, p, at which
   the results of the tests of significance were evaluated, specified
   in advance of data analysis?   _____
If parametric tests were used is there
   any evidence that one or more of
   the required assumptions were
   greatly violated?   _____
Are the tests of significance described
   appropriate, given the hypotheses
   and design of the study?   _____
Was every hypothesis tested?   _____
Are the tests of significance interpreted
   using the appropriate degrees of
   freedom?   _____
Are the results clearly presented?   _____
Are the tables and figures (if any) well
   organized and easy to understand?   _____
Are the data in each table and figure
   described in the text?   _____

Conclusions and Recommendations

CODE

Is each result discussed in terms of the
original hypothesis to which it
relates?

Is each result discussed in terms of its
agreement or disagreement with previous results obtained by other researchers in other studies? _____

Are generalizations made that are not
warranted by the results? _____

Are the possible effects of uncontrolled
variables on the results discussed? _____

Are theoretical and practical implications of the findings discussed? _____

Are recommendations for future action
made? _____

Based only on statistical significance,
are suggestions for educational action
made that are not justified by the
data; in other words, has the author
confused statistical significance
and practical significance? _____

Are recommendations for future research
made? _____

Summary (Or Abstract)

Is the problem restated? _____
Are the number and type of subjects
and instruments described? _____
Is the design used identified? _____
Are procedures described? _____
Are the major results and conclusions
restated? _____

METHOD-SPECIFIC EVALUATION CRITERIA

Identify and diagram the experimental
design used in this study:

Was an appropriate experimental design
selected? _____
Is a rationale for design selection given? _____
Are sources of invalidity associated
with the design identified and
discussed? _____
Is the method of group formation
described? _____

Was the experimental group formed in the
same way as the control group?   _____
Were existing groups used or were groups
randomly formed?   _____
Were treatments randomly assigned to
groups?   _____
Were critical extraneous variables
identified?   _____
Were any control procedures applied to
equate groups on extraneous variables?   _____
Is there any evidence to suggest reactive
arrangements (for example, the
Hawthorne effect)?   _____

Suggested Responses

CHAPTER 1

SELF-TEST FOR TASK 1-A

Are Pupils in the Open Plan School Different?

The Problem. If the (open plan) school is operating effectively, the children should show (a) more positive attitudes
toward school and themselves; (b) higher than average levels
of curiosity; and (c) higher levels of productive thinking or
"creativity."

The Procedures. Eleven and twelve-year-old pupils from four
schools in middle-class suburban Toronto took part in the
study. Two of the schools were open plan schools and two
were "traditional" schools, used as control groups; one of
the open plan schools was a "lab" school, in operation for six
years under the open plan philosophy, and the second open
plan school was new although pupils were treated under the
open plan philosophy from the start of the year. Three sets
of materials were used: a semantic differential questionnaire
to measure attitudes; the Torrance Minnesota Test of Creativity to assess productive thinking; and two curiosity questionnaires, Specific Curiosity and Reactive Curiosity to assess
curiosity. All tests were administered in the usual school
setting of the respective groups during regular school hours.

The Method of Analysis. The 21 adjectives for each concept
were subjected to a 1-way analysis of variance for the 3
groups: the lab school, new open plan school, and control
group. Mean scores for the three groups were compared using a Newman-Keuls Test with harmonic mean.

Major Conclusion(s). (1) The results generally confirm the
claims that pupils in open plan schools have better attitudes
toward school and toward themselves. (2) The higher levels
of productive thinking in a continuing open plan environment show encouraging results for the open plan philosophy.

133

(3) There were no differences among the three groups on curiosity measures.

The Objectives of Secondary School Chemistry
Teaching as Reflected in Selected
Professional Periodicals: 1918-1967

The Problem. The study was an attempt to provide a greater insight as to what information pertaining to teaching objectives was available to the classroom teacher in the form of periodical literature during the 1918-1967 period.

The Procedures. The 1918-1967 period was divided into subperiods on the basis of selected events that were judged to have had an impact on the course of American educational history. Six periodicals were selected in an attempt to represent the literature available during the time period in question; all issues of the periodicals selected were read for relevant articles and each article selected was abstracted as to its stated objectives and ideas expressed. A pilot study was undertaken to determine the workability of the project. Selected articles were read and statements (of objectives) obtained were classified into one of four categories: knowledge, process, attitude and interest, and cultural awareness.

The Method of Analysis. The information was analyzed to answer questions within and across subperiods.

The Major Conclusion. An adequate body of information reflecting concern for the development of good secondary school teaching was available to the classroom teacher during the years in question.

Immediate Knowledge of Results
and Test Performance

The Problem. The purpose of this study was to investigate the possible effect of KR (knowledge of results) on test performance.

The Procedures. The samples consisted of three groups of mathematics students: a university class for elementary school teachers, a university class in remedial mathematics, and a junior high school class in general mathematics. Students were randomly assigned to either one of two subgroups within their respective group. One subgroup in each group received KR on either the first or second half of the items on the

test; the other subgroup in each group received the opposite
condition. Each subgroup had delayed knowledge of results
(DKR) on the other half of the test items. The groups used
punchboards to receive KR. Scores on one-hour exams and a
final exam were compared for the subgroups.

The Method of Analysis. Two-way analysis of variance was
used to determine the effect of KR on student test performance.

The Major Conclusion. In general, there were no significant
differences in the results of the two methods of testing although students tended to perform better when they were
given KR.

The One-Minute Step Test as a Measure of 600-Yard Run Performance

The Problem. This study was designed to determine the
validity of various step tests as measures of 600-yard run
performance in ninth-grade girls. Those tests which provided the best prediction of performance were then studied
further for reliability and the effects of age, weight, and
height.

The Procedures. Ninth-grade girls (N = 40) enrolled in
regular physical education classes in Bloomfield, New Jersey,
served as subjects. Scores were acquired for all subjects
on the 600-yard run-walk, the Skubic-Hodgkins step test, the
one- and two-minute (four count) step test, and the one- and
two-minute (two-count) step test.

The Method of Analysis. The correlation coefficients between
the various step-up test scores and the 600-yard run time were
computed.

The Major Conclusion. The two-count one-minute step test is
a reasonably valid and reliable measure of 600-yard run
performance in junior high school girls.

135

The Professional Reading of English
Teachers in Florida

The Problem. A survey was conducted designed to test the
knowledge English teachers have of educational journals and
books.

The Procedures. A survey of reading habits was sent to 580
randomly selected teachers of English in the state of Florida.
The survey listed journal titles related to the teaching of
English, 10 journal titles related to education, and 20 book
titles in each field. Also included was a numbering system
enabling respondents to indicate the degree of their familiarity with the works listed. As a precaution against a
teacher's checking items whether he or she had read them or
not, exactly half of the journal and book titles listed were
fictitious. The anonymous survey also solicited information
about the respondents' education and teaching experience and
about their membership in professional organizations.

The Method of Analysis. Of the 580 sent, 386 completed and
usable surveys were returned. Results are presented in tables
which indicate the number of teachers selecting each code number for each publication (1 = never heard of it and progres-
sively higher numbers indicate increasingly greater degrees
of familiarity).

The Major Conclusion. Teachers of secondary school English
are not presently reading widely in professional literature,
nor have they read widely in the past.

Are Pupils in the Open Plan School Different?

Method: Causal-Comparative

Reasons: A cause-effect relationship was investigated. The
           independent variable (cause), type of school attend-
           ed (open plan versus traditional) was not manipu-
           lated. Subjects were selected who were <u>already</u>
           <u>attending</u> either an open plan school or a tradi-
           tional school. The subjects' attitudes, creativity,
           and curiosity were then compared.

The Objectives of Secondary School Chemistry
Teaching as Reflected in Selected
Professional Periodicals: 1918-1967

Method: Historical

Reasons: This research involved the study and analysis of
           past events. It was concerned with the question
           of the <u>evolution</u> of objectives as reflected by
           statements in articles from selected professional
           periodicals.

Immediate Knowledge of Results and
Test Performance

Method: Experimental

Reasons: A cause-effect relationship was investigated.
           The independent variable (cause), time of feedback
           (KR versus DKR), was manipulated. Subjects were
           randomly assigned to either one of two subgroups
           within their respective group. The subjects'
           performance on a series of examinations was then
           compared.

The One-Minute Step Test as a Measure of
600-Yard Run Performance

Method: Correlational

Reasons: A cause-effect relationship was <u>not</u> investigated.
           A relationship was investigated -- the relationship
           between performance on various step tests and
           performance on the 600-yard run. These relation-

ships were determined for purposes of prediction, i.e., to determine which step test score would best (most validly and reliably) predict time for the 600-yard run. Correlation coefficients were computed.

The Professional Reading of English Teachers in Florida

Method: Descriptive

Reasons: This study was designed to determine the current knowledge that English teachers have of educational journals and books. A survey was conducted. A questionnaire specifically constructed for the study was mailed to randomly selected teachers of English in the state of Florida. The reported response rate was 386 survey forms returned out of 580 mailed.

CHAPTER 4

SELF-TEST FOR ENABLERS 4-2, 4-4, 4-6 AND 4-7

ENABLER 4-2

Example 1

There are 150 first graders in the population and you want a random sample of 60 students.

1. Compile or obtain a list of the 150 first graders.
2. Assign each subject a number from 000-149.
3. Go to a table of random numbers and arbitrarily select a number.
4. Look at the last 3 digits of the numbers.
5. If that number is also assigned to a subject, that subject is in the sample; if not, go to the next number.
6. Continue down the table until 60 students are selected.

Example 2

There are 220 principals in the school system and you want a random sample of 40 principals.

1. Compile or obtain a list of the 220 principals.
2. Assign each principal a number from 000-219.
3. Go to a table of random number and arbitrarily select a number.
4. Look at the last 3 digits of the number.
5. If that number is also assigned to a subject, that subject is in the sample; if not go to the next number.
6. Continue down the table until 40 principals are selected.

Example 3

There are 320 students defined as gifted in the school system and you want a random sample of 50 gifted students.

1. Compile or obtain a list of the 320 gifted students.
2. Assign each gifted student a number from 000-319.
3. Go to a table of random numbers and arbitrarily select a number.
4. Look at the last 3 digits of the number.
5. If that number is also assigned to a subject, that subject is in the sample; if not go to the next number.
6. Continue down the table until 50 gifted students are selected.

ENABLER 4-4

Example 1

There are 500 twelfth-grade students in the population, you want a sample of 60 students, and you want to stratify on three levels of IQ in order to insure equal representation.

1. Administer an IQ test (or otherwise obtain IQ scores) and classify all students into one of three IQ groups (e.g., those with an IQ below 84, those with IQ between 84 and 116, and those with an IQ above 116).
2. Randomly select 20 students from each IQ group.

Example 2

There are 95 algebra I students in the population, you want a sample of 30 students, and you want to stratify a sex in order to insure equal representation of males and females.

1. Classify all the algebra I students as male or as female.
2. Randomly select 15 males and 15 females.

Example 3

There are 240 principals in the school system, you want a sample of 45 principals, and you want to stratify by level, i.e., elementary versus secondary, in order to insure proportional representation. You know that there are approximately twice as many secondary principals as elementary principals.

1. Identify all the elementary principals and all the secondary principals.
2. Randomly select 15 elementary principals and 30 secondary principals; this will give you a sample of 45 which contains twice as many secondary principals as elementary principals.

ENABLER 4-6

Example 1

There are 80 sixth-grade classrooms in the population, each classroom has an average of 30 students, and you want a sample of 180 students.

1. The number of classrooms needed = $\frac{180}{30}$ = 6.

2. Randomly select 6 classrooms from the population of 80 classrooms.

3. All the sixth graders in the 6 classrooms selected are in the sample.

Example 2

There are 75 schools in the school system, each school has an average of 50 teachers, and you want a sample of 350 teachers.

1. The number of schools needed = $\frac{350}{50}$ = 7.

2. Randomly select 7 schools from the population of 75 schools.
3. All the teachers in the 7 schools selected are in the sample.

Example 3

There are 100 kindergarten classes in the school system, each class has an average of 20 children, and you want a sample of 200 children.

1. The number of kindergarten classes needed = $\frac{200}{20}$ = 10.

2. Randomly select 10 kindergartens from the population of 100 kindergarten classes.
3. All the children in the 10 classes selected are in the sample.

ENABLER 4-7

Example 1

You have a list of 2,000 high school students and you want a sample of 200 students.

1. K = $\frac{2,000}{200}$ = 10.

2. Arbitrarily select a name at the top of the list.
3. Select every 10th name on the list until you have selected 200 students.

Example 2

You have a directory which lists the names and addresses of 12,000 teachers and you want a sample of 2,500 teachers.

1. K = $\frac{12,000}{2,500}$ = 4.8 or 5.

2. Arbitrarily select a name at the beginning of the directory.

3. Select every 5th name in the directory until you have
    selected 2,500 teachers.

Example 3

You have a list of 1,500 junior high school students and you
want a sample of 100 students.

1. $K = \dfrac{1,500}{100} = 15.$

2. Arbitrarily select a name at the top of the list.
3. Select every 15th name until you have selected 100
    students.

CHAPTER 5

SELF-TEST FOR ENABLERS 5-4 AND 5-6

ENABLER 5-4

Example 1

You want to determine the concurrent validity of a new IQ test for young children.

1. Obtain scores on an already established, valid IQ test for a large group of young children (or administer such a test if scores are not already available).
2. Administer the new IQ test to the same group.
3. Correlate the two sets of scores.
4. If the correlation is high, the new test has high concurrent validity with the already established test.

Example 2

You want to determine the concurrent validity of a new self-concept scale for junior high school students.

1. Obtain scores on an already established, valid self-concept scale for a large group of junior high school students (or administer such a test if scores are not already available).
2. Administer the new self-concept scale to the same group.
3. Correlate the two sets of scores.
4. If the correlation is high, the new scale has high concurrent validity with the already established scale.

Example 3

You want to determine the concurrent validity of a new reading comprehension test for high school students.

1. Obtain scores on an already established, valid test of reading comprehension for a large group of high school students (or administer such a test if scores are not already available).
2. Administer the new reading comprehension test to the same group.
3. Correlate the two sets of scores.
4. If the correlation is high, the new scale has high concurrent validity with the already established test.

Example 1

You want to predict success in graduate school and you want
to determine the predictive validity of the GRE.

1. Administer the GRE to a large group of students entering
    graduate school.
2. Collect data on the criterion measure, a valid index of
    success in graduate school such as GPA at the time of
    graduation.
3. Correlate the two sets of data.
4. If the correlation is high, the GRE has high predictive
    validity with respect to success in graduate school.

Example 2

You want to predict level of achievement in algebra I and you
want to determine the predictive validity of an algebra I
aptitude test.

1. Administer the algebra aptitude test to a large group of
    students who are going to take algebra I.
2. Collect data on the criterion measure, a valid index of
    level of achievement in algebra I such as final exam
    scores or final average.
3. Correlate the two sets of data.
4. If the correlation is high, the algebra I aptitude test
    has high predictive validity with respect to level of
    achievement in algebra I.

Example 3

You want to predict success in nursing school and you want to
determine the predictive validity of a nursing aptitude test.

1. Administer the nursing aptitude test to a large group of
    students who are entering nursing school.
2. Collect data on the criterion measure, a valid index of
    success in nursing school such as scores on a final
    performance test.
3. Correlate the two sets of scores.
4. If the correlation is high, the nursing aptitude test
    has high predictive validity with respect to success in
    nursing school.

CHAPTER 7

SELF-TEST FOR ENABLERS 7-12 AND 7-32

ENABLER 7-12

$\underline{X}$	$\underline{X^2}$
2	4
4	16
4	16
5	25
6	36
6	36
6	36
7	49
8	64
9	81
$\sum X = 57$	$\sum X^2 = 363$

$$\bar{X} = \frac{\sum X}{N} = \frac{57}{10} = \underline{\underline{5.7}}$$

$$SD = \sqrt{\frac{\sum X^2 - \frac{(\sum X)^2}{N}}{N}} = \sqrt{\frac{363 - \frac{(57)^2}{10}}{10}} = \sqrt{\frac{363 - \frac{3249}{10}}{10}}$$

$$= \sqrt{\frac{363 - 324.9}{10}} = \sqrt{\frac{38.1}{10}} = \sqrt{3.81} = \underline{\underline{1.95}}$$

$\underline{X}$	$\underline{Y}$	$\underline{X^2}$	$\underline{Y^2}$	$\underline{XY}$
2	6	4	36	12
4	6	16	36	24
4	7	16	49	28
5	8	25	64	40
6	9	36	81	54
21	36	97	266	158
ΣX	ΣY	ΣX^2	ΣY^2	ΣXY

$$\underline{r} = \frac{\Sigma XY - \frac{(\Sigma X)(\Sigma Y)}{N}}{\sqrt{\left[\Sigma X^2 - \frac{(\Sigma X)^2}{N}\right]\left[\Sigma Y^2 - \frac{(\Sigma Y)^2}{N}\right]}} = \frac{158 - \frac{(21)(36)}{5}}{\sqrt{\left[97 - \frac{(21)^2}{5}\right]\left[266 - \frac{(36)^2}{5}\right]}}$$

$$= \frac{158 - \frac{756}{5}}{\sqrt{\left[97 - \frac{441}{5}\right]\left[266 - \frac{(1296)}{5}\right]}} = \frac{158 - 151.2}{\sqrt{\left[97 - 88.2\right]\left[266 - 259.2\right]}}$$

$$= \frac{6.8}{\sqrt{\left[8.8\right]\left[6.8\right]}} = \frac{6.8}{\sqrt{59.84}} = \frac{6.8}{7.74} = .8786$$

$$\underline{r} = \underline{\underline{.88}}$$

$$z_1 = \frac{X - \overline{X}}{SD} = \frac{2 - 5.7}{1.95}$$

$$= \frac{-3.7}{1.95} = \underline{\underline{-1.90}}$$

$$z_2 = \frac{X - \overline{X}}{SD} = \frac{4 - 5.7}{1.95}$$

$$= \frac{-1.7}{1.95} = \underline{\underline{-.87}}$$

$$z_3 = \frac{X - \overline{X}}{SD} = \frac{4 - 5.7}{1.95}$$

$$= \frac{-1.7}{1.95} = \underline{\underline{-.87}}$$

$$z_4 = \frac{X - \overline{X}}{SD} = \frac{5 - 5.7}{1.95}$$

$$= \frac{-.7}{1.95} = \underline{\underline{-.36}}$$

$$z_5 = \frac{X - X}{SD} = \frac{6 - 5.7}{1.95}$$

$$\frac{.3}{1.95} = \underline{\underline{+.15}}$$

$$z_6 = \frac{X - \overline{X}}{SD} = \frac{6 - 5.7}{1.95}$$

$$= \frac{.3}{1.95} = \underline{\underline{+.15}}$$

$$z_7 = \frac{X - \overline{X}}{SD} = \frac{6 - 5.7}{1.95}$$

$$= \frac{.3}{1.95} = \underline{\underline{+.15}}$$

$$z_8 = \frac{X - \overline{X}}{SD} = \frac{7 - 5.7}{1.95}$$

$$= \frac{1.3}{1.95} = \underline{\underline{+.67}}$$

$$z_9 = \frac{X - \overline{X}}{SD} = \frac{8 - 5.7}{1.95}$$

$$= \frac{2.3}{1.95} = \underline{\underline{+1.18}}$$

$$z_{10} = \frac{X - \overline{X}}{SD} = \frac{9 - 5.7}{1.95}$$

$$= \frac{3.3}{1.95} = \underline{\underline{+1.69}}$$

147

X_1	X_2	X_3
2	3	7
3	3	8
4	4	8
5	5	8
7	6	9

$\underline{t}$ test for independent samples

X_1	χ_1	χ_1^2	X_2	χ_2	χ_2^2
2	-2.2	4.84	3	-1.2	1.44
3	-1.2	1.44	3	-1.2	1.44
4	- .2	.04	4	- .2	.04
5	+ .8	.64	5	+ .8	.64
7	+2.8	7.84	6	+1.8	3.24
$\overline{21}$		$\overline{14.80}$	$\overline{21}$		$\overline{6.80}$

$$\Sigma x_1 \qquad\qquad \Sigma \chi_1^2 \quad \Sigma x_2$$

$$\overline{X}_1 = \frac{\Sigma x_1}{n_1} = \frac{21}{5} = 4.2 \qquad\qquad \overline{X}_2 = \frac{\Sigma x_2}{n_2} = \frac{21}{5} = 4.2$$

$$t = \frac{\overline{X}_1 - \overline{X}_2}{\sqrt{\left(\dfrac{X_1^2 + X\Sigma_2^2}{n_1 + n_2 - 2}\right)\left(\dfrac{1}{n_1} + \dfrac{1}{n_2}\right)}} = \frac{4.2 - 4.2}{\sqrt{\left(\dfrac{14.8 + 6.8}{5 + 5 - 2}\right)\left(\dfrac{1}{5} + \dfrac{1}{5}\right)}}$$

$$= \frac{0}{\sqrt{\left(\dfrac{21.6}{8}\right)\left(\dfrac{2}{5}\right)}} = \frac{0}{\sqrt{(2.7)(.4)}} = \frac{0}{\sqrt{1.08}} = \frac{0}{1.04} = 0$$

$\underline{t} = 0$

$\underline{df} = n_1 + n_2 - 2 = 5 + 5 - 2 = 8$

$p = .05$

$\underline{t} = 0$ is less than 2.306 (See Table A.4)

Therefore, there is no significant difference between the two groups.

$\underline{t}$ test for nonindependent samples

X_2	X_3	D	D^2
3	7	+4	16
3	8	+5	25
4	8	+4	16
5	8	+3	9
6	9	+3	9
		$\dfrac{+3}{19}$ $\sum D$	$\dfrac{9}{75}$ $\sum D^2$

$$\overline{D} = \frac{\sum D}{N} = \frac{19}{5} = 3.8$$

$$\underline{t} = \frac{\overline{D}}{\sqrt{\dfrac{\sum D^2 - \dfrac{(\sum D)^2}{N}}{N(N-1)}}} = \frac{3.8}{\sqrt{\dfrac{75 - \dfrac{(19)^2}{5}}{5(5-1)}}}$$

$$= \frac{3.8}{\sqrt{\dfrac{75 - \dfrac{361}{5}}{5(4)}}} = \frac{3.8}{\sqrt{\dfrac{75 - 72.2}{20}}} = \frac{3.8}{\sqrt{\dfrac{2.8}{2.0}}}$$

$$= \frac{3.8}{\sqrt{.14}} = \frac{3.8}{.37} = 10.27$$

$\underline{t} = 10.27$; $\underline{df} = n - 1 = 5 - 1 = 4$; $\underline{p} = .05$

$\underline{t} = 10.27$ is greater than 2.776 (See Table A.4)

Therefore, there is a significant difference between the two groups.

Simple analysis of variance for 3 groups

X_1	X_1^2	X_2	X_2^2	X_3	X_3^2
2	4	3	9	7	49
3	9	3	9	8	64
4	16	4	16	8	64
5	25	5	25	8	64
7	49	6	36	9	81
21	103	21	95	40	322
$\sum X_1$	$\sum X_1^2$	$\sum X_2$	$\sum X_2^2$	$\sum X_3$	$\sum X_3^2$

$$SS_{total} = SS_{between} + SS_{within}$$

$$SS_{between} = \frac{(\sum X_1)^2}{n_1} + \frac{(\sum X_2)^2}{n_2} + \frac{(\sum X_3)^2}{n_3} - \frac{(\sum X)^2}{N}$$

$$= \frac{(21)^2}{5} + \frac{(21)^2}{5} + \frac{(40)^2}{5} - \frac{(82)^2}{15}$$

$$= \frac{441}{5} + \frac{441}{5} + \frac{1,600}{5} - \frac{6,724}{15}$$

$$= 88.2 + 88.2 + 320 - 448.27$$

$$= 496.4 - 448.27 = \underline{48.13}$$

$$SS_{total} = \sum X^2 - \frac{(\sum X)^2}{N} = 520 - 448.27 = \underline{71.73}$$

$$SS_{within} = SS_{total} - SS_{between}$$

$$= 71.73 - 48.13 = \underline{23.60}$$

SOURCE OF VARIATION	SUM OF SQUARES	df		MEAN SQUARES	F
Between	48.13	(K-1)	2	24.06	12.21
Within	23.60	(N-K)	12	1.97	
Total	71.73	(N-1)	14		

F = 12.21; df = 2, 12; p = .05

F = 12.21 is greater than 3.88 (See Table A.5)

Therefore, there is a significant difference among the groups.

152

Duncan's new multiple range test

$$SE_{\bar{x}} = \frac{s}{\sqrt{n}} \qquad\qquad s = \sqrt{MS_w}$$

n = number of subjects in each group

$$= \frac{\sqrt{1.97}}{\sqrt{5}} = \frac{1.40}{2.24} = .62$$

Significant studentized ranges (See Table A.6) are 4.32 and 4.50.

Shortest significant ranges, R_2 and R_3

$$R_2 = (4.32)(.62) \qquad\qquad R_3 = (4.50)(.62)$$
$$= 2.68 \qquad\qquad\qquad\qquad = 2.79$$

$$\bar{x}_1 = \frac{21}{5} = 4.2 \qquad \bar{x}_2 = \frac{21}{5} = 4.2 \qquad \bar{x}_3 = \frac{40}{5} = 8.0$$

	Means	$\bar{x}_1$ 4.2	$\bar{x}_2$ 4.2	$\bar{x}_3$ 8.0	Shortest Significant Ranges
$\bar{x}_1$	4.2		0.0	3.8	2.68 = R_2
$\bar{x}_2$	4.2			3.8	2.79 = R_3

0.0 $\ngtr$ 2.68, therefore there is not a significant difference between $\bar{x}_1$ and $\bar{x}_2$.

3.8 > 2.68, therefore there is a significant difference between $\bar{x}_1$ and $\bar{x}_3$.

3.8 > 2.79, therefore there is a significant difference between $\bar{x}_2$ and $\bar{x}_3$.

Chi square χ^2

Responses

	Yes	No	Undecided
observed	21	21	40
expected	27.3	27.3	27.3

total: 82

(Note: expected $= \dfrac{82}{3} = 27.3$)

$$\chi^2 = \sum \left[\frac{(fo - fe)^2}{fe} \right]$$

$$\chi^2 = \frac{(21 - 27.3)^2}{27.3} + \frac{(21 - 27.3)^2}{27.3} + \frac{(40 - 27.3)^2}{27.3}$$

$$= \frac{(-6.3)^2}{27.3} + \frac{(-6.3)^2}{27.3} + \frac{(12.7)^2}{27.3}$$

$$= \frac{39.69}{27.3} + \frac{39.69}{27.3} + \frac{161.29}{27.3}$$

$$= 1.45 + 1.45 + 5.91 = \underline{8.81}$$

$\chi^2 = 8.81;$ $\underline{df} = K - 1 = 3 - 1 = 2;$ $\underline{p} = .05$

$\chi^2 = 8.81 > 5.991$ (See Table A.7)

Therefore, there is a significant difference between observed and expected frequencies.

Immediate Knowledge of Results
and Test Performance

GENERAL EVALUATION CRITERIA

Introduction

Problem   CODE

    A statement?   Y
        Paragraph (¶) 1, last sentence(s)
    Researchable?   Y
    Background information?   Y
        Minimal; ¶1, S 1 & 2
    Significance discussed?   Y
        Briefly; ¶1, S 3 & 4
    Variables and relationships stated?   Y
    Definitions?   N
        KR and DKR are perhaps discussed
        implicitly (a punchboard was used),
        but not explicitly; "punchboard" is
        not described.

Review of Related Literature

    Comprehensive?   N
    References relevant?   Y
    Sources primary?   Y
    Critical analysis?   N
    Well-organized?   N
    Summary?   N
    Rational for hypotheses?   NA
Note: The review is so limited that it is
      difficult to answer the above questions.

Hypotheses

    Questions or hypotheses?   N
    Expected difference stated?   NA
    Variables defined?   NA
    Testable?   NA
Note: Since the answer to the first question is N,
      the remainder of the questions become NA.

Method

Subjects

Population described?	N
Entire population used?	N
Sample selected?	Y
Method described?	N
Sample representative?	?
Volunteers?	N

Sample described?
      It is only stated what kinds of students
      were used; under Method, ¶ 1, S 1 & 2.

Minimum size?	0

Instruments

Rationale for selection?	NA

      Apparently self-developed tests were
      used; under Method, ¶'s 2 & 3.

Instruments described?	N
Appropriate?	?
Procedures for development described?	N
Evidence that appropriate for sample?	N
Validity discussed?	N
Reliability discussed?	N
Subtest reliabilities?	NA
Administrating, scoring, and interpretation procedures described?	N

Design and Procedure

Design appropriate?	Y
Procedures sufficiently detailed?	N
Pilot study?	N
Description of pilot study?	NA
Control procedures described?	N
Confounding variables not controlled?	Y

      For example, the Hawthorne effect and
      the novelty effect

Results

Appropriate descriptive statistics?	Y
Probability level specified in advance?	Y

      Under Results; ¶ 1, S 3

Parametric assumptions violated?	X
Tests of significance appropriate?	NA

      Because no hypotheses

Appropriate degrees of freedom?	X

Results clearly presented?   Y
Tables and figures well organized?   Y
Data in each table and figure described?   Y

Conclusions and Recommendations

Results discussed in terms of hypotheses?   NA
Results discussed in terms of previous
      research?   N
Unwarranted generalizations?   N
Effects of uncontrolled variables discussed?   N
Implications discussed?   N
Recommendations for action?   Y
      Under Discussion, ¶2
Confusion of practical and statistical
      significance?   Y
      The mean difference on the final exam
      was only 1.70 (28.97 - 27.27); maximum
      score on each test is not even
      mentioned.
Recommendations for research?   N

Summary (Or Abstract)

Problem restated?   Y
Subjects and instrument described?   N
Design identified?   Y
Procedures?   Y
Results and conclusions?   Y

METHOD-SPECIFIC EVALUATION CRITERIA

Design used:

Subgroup 1	$X_1 0$	$X_2 0$	$X_1 =$ KR
Subgroup 2	$X_2 0$	$X_1 0$	$X_2 =$ DKR

      Basically a counterbalanced design with
      both subgroups receiving both treatments
      but on different rotating halves of tests
      (See Method, ¶1, last 4 S's).

Design appropriate   Y
Selection rationale?   N
Invalidity discussed?   N

Group formation described?   <u>Y</u>
    Under Method, ¶1, S 3.
Groups formed in same way?   <u>Y</u>
Groups randomly formed?   <u>Y</u>
    Subgroups were
Treatments randomly assigned?   <u>NA</u>
Extraneous variables described?   <u>N</u>
Groups equated?   <u>NA</u>
    Both groups received both treatments.
Reactive arrangements?   <u>Y</u>
    Hawthorne effect and novelty effect.